The Path

The Essene Legacy
BOOK THREE

Channeled by Al Miner and Lama Sing

Cover art and book design by Susan Miner

Second Edition 2016

Library of Congress Control Number: 2010911131

ISBN -978-0-9791262-9-1
ISBN-10-9791262-9-0
1. Spirit writings 2. Psychics 3. Trance Channels 4. Essenes
4. Expectant Ones 5. Jesus Christ 6. The Promise
I. Miner, Al II. Title

Printed in the United States of America

For books and products or to write to Al Miner, visit:
www.lamasing.net

to the Promise

CONTENTS

About These Works
About Al Miner

Chapter One

In the School of the Prophets

Jesus and the children who have been sent with Him from the Essene encampment in the Three Holy Mountains have arrived at the School of the Prophets. It is the adept Daniel who steps forward from the large entourage greeting the children. He pauses for a few moments to look about the sizeable gathering of these young wards.

"Welcome to our sanctuary," he begins. "We call it a school because we are all learning and sharing. As we pledge to give you the truth as we see it, the knowledge and insights that we have come to know to be good, we invite you to give your truths unto us. While many here come from differing lands and will appear foreign to you, remember that you are to them as they are to you. Look around and ask us, and we shall guide you to all that we are and all that we have here.

"We have no rules, no conditions, no mandates. We come together to celebrate and to offer our prayers because we are so guided from within. We find joy in so doing. Any of these brothers and sisters will give you as you ask of them. And know this, it is their prayer that you *will* ask. For is it not, dear brothers and sisters, the greatest of all joys when one is asked to give? For in the giving comes the receipt of even greater blessings. And as one's inner cup is filled to overflowing, even greater shall be given.

"We have prepared nourishment for you and believe you will discover some of your favorite foods there. After you have dined, we invite you to choose whatever quarter you will that brings gladness to your heart." Daniel extends his arm pointing towards the sides, behind, and higher into the reaches where narrow pathways disappear. He then turns back to the faces before him. "Any chamber is yours for the asking. We will begin our work together in the morning after your meal and the night's good rest."

The delectable aromas of various foods have reached the children, so a nod and smile from Daniel is all they need. They jump up, rushing into position for their prayer of thanksgiving and, chattering gaily among themselves and with their new teachers, begin their evening meal.

"It has to do with the positioning of each of you," the prophet begins quietly, as he seats the students in curious patterns. "There are natural laws and eternal laws, laws which govern all things," he continues. "The knowledge of these provides the opportunity to do works within them, to flow with them, and, yes, even to divert the intentions of others who would limit you or cause you harm."

Daniel walks around the group, here and there repositioning the posture of some of the young Essenes on this their first morning in the sacred School.

"Look to your body," he instructs one of the younger maidens. "It is an instrument of your inner intent. If your body looks careless or is disoriented or imbalanced in any way, then it generates that kind of energy.

"Begin within yourself and bring the energy and light upwards and let your body indicate that you have done so. Do not let it indicate that you are lax, that there is any weakness, or doubt.

"Be as the Staff of God. Be strong! If you emanate this physically, it will be the power that the observer will perceive. You must establish the initial advantage, for if you are seeking to do a work, whether it be healing or defense of any sort, this first step quite often determines the outcome! Mind you, you shall not remain idle after this lesson, but it is a very important one. And we shall do this again and again, day after day, month after month, year after year, if need be, until you manifest what I know is possible for you."

Other adepts of the School are also moving about the group, adjusting postures and gently guiding the students.

Just as it was earlier that day, later on, when night has fallen, one of the adepts is teaching.

"Look over here." He points to the heavens. "See this alignment?" He walks about, aided by his brothers and sisters from the School. "These never change. They are constant. When you find one, look for the others, for they will tell you much. If you cannot see which route your journey is to take, they will tell you. They will guide you unto that which is in answer to your prayer. First, though, you must find those that are as the rod or staff of God … always present. They will point you to the answer you seek. Certain ones are like the guardians of your peoples … constant, impervious to all else. Others," he gestures more broadly to the evening's star-filled sky, "are in motion, transient, providing the seeker with the answers to other queries."

Again the adepts position the group, which includes the Master. In the years ahead He will call many of the children who are on the first stages of their journey, and still more who have been as brothers and sisters to Him during the nurturing of His Spirit's Light while His heritage was being awakened.

All the students are pondering, reflecting. For the gifts of these Magi are incomparable. The many gifts of the seers, the prophecies and truths that are offered, are being given in a constant stream. Much of what had been familiar to the young Expectant Ones' – rituals, daily works and blessings – is now absent, for many of these adepts follow different paths, offer different prayers, and, clearly, do many different works.

"Walk this way," Daniel instructs James strictly, yet with understanding. He seems to be following an imaginary line as each of the young adepts and the Master watch him carefully.

"Hold the thoughts that I gave you. Now, watch!" Daniel moves slowly around the circumference of the group, truly a great space, indeed, so large that many of those with the Master wonder about it. Their custom had been to form in geometrical patterns of such proximity that one could reach a hand out and touch a brother or sister. But now, many paces separate the children from those to their left and right. And some are higher, some lower. It is strange, indeed.

A moment later, we hear a soft chant begin in the upper reaches of one of the craggy rock outcroppings that constitute the walls of the School's inner chamber. Daniel's arms and hands come up. He brings them in front of himself as he walks very slowly, as if measuring each step, one foot in front of the other. The chanting seems to be in concert with the movement of his hands and arms.

His hands come together, arms outstretched in front of him, fingertips touching. We hear him murmur something almost inaudible. Slowly his hands turn over until their backs are one to the other.

The chanting crescendos. It is melodic, almost hypnotic. As Daniel takes another step, his hands begin to part, moving outward as though grasping something, as if time and space consisted of a fabric that his hands are now seizing. As he continues these measured steps forward, his pace increases and his hands and arms move the invisible curtain before him.

Then Daniel disappears!

Many murmur *oo-o* and *ah-h.* Several offer brief prayers to God.

But Daniel is no more.

Some students rub their faces, their eyes, as if testing to see, *Have we been charmed? Has there been some spell?*

What is this?

Many of the adepts move about silently, watching all of those who have come from the Essene lands, studying them carefully.

One adept, standing before the Master, duly notes a gentle smile and a light shining in His eyes. "Your Spirit knows this, then?" he asks softly.

Jesus nods, smiling. "I know it."

"Would you come forward?"

"If it is purposeful, yes."

The adept reaches out to take the Master's hand. The two then make their way to the center of the group where Daniel had begun his curious walk forward. Yet, he is still not to be seen.

"Here," the Master affirms and stops, releasing the adept's hand.

As He glances around, the Master receives warm smiles. The love of this group for Him is clearly unquestionable.

The adept, who is now ten to fifteen paces away from Him, asks a bit more loudly, "Is there any need you have?"

Smiling, the Master fixes His eyes upon the adept, whose face immediately fills with a great smile. He merely nods, for he realizes that Jesus needs naught.

The Master brings His hands up before Him for just a moment. He bows His head, His chin touching the forefingers of His hands, which are clasped together. Perhaps a mere handful of seconds passes, so brief, then His hands come down. He opens His eyes, lifts His head, and begins to walk. Not in the manner as Daniel did, not gesturing with His hands or arms, but slowly, ever so casually, His face aglow with a warm smile.

Suddenly, He, too, vanishes!

Again, outcries echo about the entire group.

A few moments later, the group is astounded to see the Master returning from the nothingness, serenely walking the path He had trod only moments ago.

Behind Him several paces away, smiling and nodding, looking this way and that, Daniel follows. Hands together and face aglow, he begins to laugh aloud.

The Master turns around, walks over, and embraces him.

"Look you, one and all," Daniel begins. "It is not trickery, nor illusion, but faith. Just as you saw me go, did you see this, your Brother, whom some call Jesus, whom others call by differing names, come and bring me back into the world of the living? How can this be?

"If you can see me not, do I not exist? If the flesh and the temple that house the eternal Self are no longer visible to you, am I naught? Your Brother Jesus knows, for God speaks to Him and guides Him. They are one. If you believe in the teachings that lie ahead, we shall show you, and invite from Him even greater. But think now upon this:

"When that time comes when He is not among you, as He has just moments ago not been among you, can you call Him forth? Can you call me forth? Can you call forth the brothers and sisters of your peoples who ever hold you in prayer and meditation? Can you? Yes, you can if you believe. You can if your faith does not give way to illusion or temptation. In the heavens and Earth alike, in the experiences, the challenges, God is ever with you, as are each of us because we so choose.

"Now as you prepare for slumber, open yourself to receive that guidance that is unto your individual need. But in this work here, this day and this evening, remember: All of this and greater shall we do."

It is not that one must travel a path alone.

But as one does move into that oneness here and there they can oft become the better, the stronger, the more prepared to move hand in hand with their brothers and sisters.

As a journey might take them this way and that, and they perhaps find themselves in need, seemingly alone, they can open themselves, just as given above, and claim the power and oneness of that which has been by the measure of time, but shall always be through faith in oneness with God.

That is our prayer for you.

Chapter Two

Rainbow of Life

They are quite scattered as they sleep, well into the wee hours. No light shines forth save the illumination of the stars, yet it is sufficient for one to see. For the clarity of the sky here in the area of the School of the Prophets is consummate, clear beyond that which one can imagine, for the air is still, and naught is present to obscure the beauty of the heavens.

One young figure stirs this way and that. Finally, he rubs his eyes and sits upright looking about, realizing that the hour is yet early. Contemplating for a moment or two the dreams he has just visited, he decides to arise. Quietly gathering and fastening his sandals on his feet and reaching for his outer garment, he covers himself and rises, careful not to touch any of his brethren who are sleeping nearby.

In the distance, embers of various cookfires glow dimly, not yet fueled for the morning's meal. He moves slowly. Once past the array of sleeping brethren, he quickly proceeds down a small passageway, tightening his outer garment and bringing it up close beneath his chin and over his head. He looks into the edge of the darkness. Casting an eye upwards, he smiles as he recognizes the celestial patterns and remembers the teachings. He follows the design, the pattern, knowing that in so doing he can find the area of the great School that he has yet to explore.

He moves easily. Noting a very rough pathway that leads gently upwards, he decides to follow it. The further he journeys, the more difficult the way becomes. Finally, he scours about for handholds and footholds to continue his climb, feeling as he does a stirring of excitement, feeling as if the stars above are reaching down to embrace him as he strives to climb closer and closer to them.

In his mind he turns over many stories, accountings of the Ancient Ones. Pausing for a moment at a bit of widening in his chosen path, he looks about and offers a silent prayer. He smiles as he recalls the wondrous stories, the great testimonies of courage and faith. These warm him. He slips the garment off of his head to feel more at ease, unrestricted, and then moves steadily upward with greater and greater vigor.

The last few meters are the most difficult. He can feel the strain on his young muscles as he slowly pulls himself up to find a beautiful vista, a sizeable plateau, relatively flat and unobstructed. Getting to his feet, he spreads his arms wide, turning about, looking at the panoramic view of a vast array of stars that flash and dance as if celebrating his ascension to this astonishing place.

He moves off, following the plateau's irregular shape, moving, moving upwards, sometimes slowly, sometimes having to climb over large fallen boulders on the plateau's surface. Finally, he comes to the end of this formation of majestic stones, thrust up out of the earth as though some great finger of Nature herself were pointing, *This way unto God.* As he comes to the edge, he looks down. The distance below is dizzying, but it is marked by that same orange-red glow of the small fires that he left not that long ago. He seats himself close to the edge where he can look down and out across the horizon. Folding his arms, he covers his body securely and prays. "If I am to serve Thee, Lord God, how shall I know that which is Thy intent? How shall I choose which path is that which Thou wouldst have me follow? I open myself here in this sanctuary of oneness with Thee. Guide me, strengthen me that I might serve my Brother to the fullest."

We hear the traditional rustle of all of the brothers and sisters awakening, young and old. Some are already dutifully about the cookfires, fueling them.

To the distance we hear chanting as some celebrate a new day of opportunity for their spirits to grow and be as a light to others in the Earth, the rhythmic striking of metallic-like sacred symbols intertwining with their chants.

Down below a bit another group is gathered, arms locked, chanting in a rhythmic, singsong pattern, peering into a new fire created solely for this purpose. The young brother and sister Essenes have assembled and are striving to emulate that which they have been taught up to this point is good. While they are awkward in some ways, even clumsy in others, the essence of what they have known throughout the years shines brilliantly in their eyes.

Their group prayer is complete, as are the purification rituals that most here practice. They have taken nourishment, and several of the elders who are adepts in the School are moving around asking about those who have had visions and dreams, pausing here and there to help with interpretation, and encouraging those who have had none to consider that, too, as a gift of God. The adepts offer insights and answers to questions that flow in a steady stream.

"One is missing," Daniel remarks to several of the others.

"Yes. We have asked Iliam to seek him out."

"Which is it?"

"It is John."

Daniel's eyebrows arch as a flash of emotion crosses his face. "Where can he be?"

"We only know, good teacher, that he is safe. We feel his spirit and it shines."

As they seat themselves to meditate, they are startled when a small pebble clanks against a large pot nearby. Turning this way and that, one of the younger adepts finally begins to laugh aloud and points upward.

All turn to see way above them a pair of feet dangling over the edge of the cliff and a hand waving.

Exuberance fills the wadis, as all laugh with mixed emotions of relief, joy, and humor.

Then, very swiftly another figure can be seen. It is Iliam.

John turns to look up and sees Iliam smiling, but with a hint of authority.

John quickly counters it. "I could not sleep. I felt called and so I answered the call. That is correct, is it not?"

Iliam still smiles as he rocks to and fro on his heels. "Well, it is correct, but you could have awakened one of us."

"For what purpose? Had you heard the call, you would have awakened of your own accord, and not required me to awaken you."

Iliam is struck with both a note of humor and respect for the authority in this young man.

John carefully rises and brushes his garments, turns to wave below to indicate all is well, and reaches out his hand.

Iliam takes it and they begin to walk.

Carefully moving back over the path that John had followed earlier, Iliam guides him to another way of descending the high mount. "I suspect you will find, little brother, that this path is considerably easier than the one you traveled."

"I knew not of its presence," John replies, to reauthorize himself, so to speak. "Whence I came was in darkness, now it is light. So it *is* considerably easier, you are correct. If it occurs again, I shall remember it. Thank you."

Iliam shakes his head, laughing to himself, for clearly this one will not be fettered by any rule, by any authority, save that which he decides is righteous. "Tell me of your call, John."

"It was strong, strange. It began as visions, as dreams. I was standing in water, very cold, to here," he adds, gesturing to his midsection. "I was alone. Others, many others, looked at me, but I knew not why. They neither joined me, nor told me to come forth from the water. Then I thought that the water must be something to indicate the Spirit of God, and I asked myself, *John, standest thou alone in the Spirit of God?* But I knew this was not so. I have in my company, now in my life, beautiful brothers and sisters and all of you, Iliam, and the others whose spirits shine so brightly that it dazzles my eyes to look upon you at times."

Smiling, Iliam squeezes John's hand in response, and nods.

"Yet there I was. I saw myself as though I were someone else. Then I looked through my eyes and saw myself. How very curious that was. How very enlightening. When I realized I could do either, I chose to look upon myself and not be bound by flesh. When I did so I saw my Brother Jesus as I was … you know, not in flesh but in the light form. Then I saw others and they were all with Him. I smiled and laughed and called to Him, and He gestured to me."

John falls silent.

As they reach the bottom of the mount, turning to ascend the narrow passageway that leads to the encampment, Iliam asks gently, "What then?"

John looks down and then off to the side. "I wanted to join them, but I could not. For some reason I had to go back, and I found myself back in the body of flesh, in the cold water, looking. I knew that I was speaking, but I heard not my own words. I awoke troubled. I felt it was a call of God. I did not wish to go back into the cold water in dream or vision, so I chose to remain awake. And I felt guided to move closer to God. That is why I sought this mount, this high place." He points up to whence they had just come.

Grasping Iliam's hand more tightly, John stops and turns

to look up at him, for Iliam is of considerable stature. "Please know that I meant no concern or lack of respect. I meant only to serve … to serve God and to answer what I believe, even as I speak to you, was and is a call."

Iliam bends and comes to one knee, placing his hands on John's shoulders, and looks at him. "On behalf of all my brothers and sisters of this great School, I say to you, young John, we are always with you and would ever support you and your judgments. If you believe that you were called by God, then that is sufficient unto itself and none will find fault with it. Know, rather, that I and my brethren salute you."

For several long moments John looks into Iliam's warm and loving eyes, then at his somewhat curious garb. Slowly he brings his arms up and embraces Iliam mightily. "I and my spirit thank you for the gladness of heart that has just been your gift to me." He moves back, releasing his hold, and places a hand on one side of Iliam's face. "May our Lord God ever bless you with the strength, the clarity of spirit and mind, that I now see shining from the center of your being. May He gift you with the power to bring it forward to others, as you have just gifted it to me."

Wordlessly, John turns, tugging on Iliam, urging him to hurriedly get back on his feet, and so he does. Soon they are greeted warmly, enthusiastically, by all of the goodly number who have gathered here.

Daniel strides over to greet John and Iliam, saluting them in the tradition of his people. "How was your journey, John?"

"I would say very fruitful, although I have questions that I would like to ask when it is appropriate."

A bit amused by John's boldness, Daniel manages to maintain his serene composure. "It is always the right time for your questions. Let us gather with the rest of your brothers and sisters and you may present them. We have been discussing the dreams, visions, and guidance that the others have received. I am sure they will wish to know of your adventure and hear your questions. Is this acceptable?"

"I should find that most joyful." John smiles and follows Daniel.

Off and behind their previous position is a gentle slope that seems to be the favorite of many of the adepts in the School. They are all settled there now and conversations are taking place in small groups.

Daniel raises his hand and calls out for all to come into oneness. They swiftly comply. "Your dreams and visions have been most fruitful, as many of my brothers and sisters have conveyed to me. They are indicative of your progress and foretell, as well, what lies ahead. It is important that each of you remembers that God is not distant but ever with us and that in the time of our body's sleep we can hear, see, and know His guidance, perhaps as clearly as we might ever seek."

A hand comes up over to the right. Noting it, Daniel responds, "If you will hold your question for a moment, I have promised John, here, that we would hear his first, and then we shall come to yours. Is this acceptable?"

Moira nods, her bright smile shining on everyone.

A silence follows as all wait for John to formulate his questions. He looks down, studying the earth beneath his feet. "My question is this … I can look upon each of you and when I ask God to awaken my sight of your spirit, I see your light and it is beautiful to behold. In that same sight, I can turn this way and that and see the light of the Spirit of God in all things. When I am asleep and have a vision, guidance from God, as I have just experienced this night past, I do not always understand, and it would seem oft times that what I seek is only given in part. Other parts seems to be withheld, or beyond my ability to perceive. My question is, *why*? What am I to do to make my perception and ability fuller, as I know God intends for all of us, so I can know these things and not be limited in any wise when God is speaking."

A pronounced silence follows, for the question bears within it the presumption that all can do this, that all know it.

Some of the adepts lean to whisper to one another.

As Iliam touches John on the shoulder, he instantly turns to smile at his new companion. "Is it possible, John, that the things that you seek, that lie beyond what you seem able to perceive, are not to be seen or known in the present?"

"Why?"

Iliam, at first taken aback by the directness of the question, glances up at Daniel with a smile and receiving one in return, along with a nod, looks back at John. "Knowing all of the future at times might be a burden, and not a joy."

John scrutinizes Iliam. "I have no fear of the burden of knowing the future, although occasionally I do feel some emotion, that is true." He glances around at the rest of his group who know intimately of what he speaks. "But if I am to know which path, what choices to make in life, it seems important to know what lies ahead and which path takes me to that which is purposeful and according to God's Will."

Iliam looks about, studying the faces. His eyes come to rest upon young Jesus who is smiling and looking at John, nodding when he speaks, then turning to Iliam when he answers. The softness in His eyes shows Iliam instantly that Jesus knows and feels just as John does. Yet, peace is evident in Him. "You are his brother," Iliam calls over to Jesus. "Might you find it in your guidance to answer John?"

Jesus cants His head, catching the eye of John, who instantly flashes a smile. Placing one hand on the ground, Jesus spryly comes to His feet and, without invitation, strides in between his brothers and sisters to seat Himself directly before John, Daniel to His left, Iliam to His right.

The Master stretches out His right hand to John, palm up. John reaches over with his right hand to place it upon the Master's. Their eyes lock in friendship, in spirit, and in a form of communion that all who perceive them realize is on a wondrously deep, spiritual level.

"To answer my brother, that which was unanswered in your vision, the prophecy, we must yet fulfill. Thus I did not call you to us, for that is the prophecy and the work before us, our holy work. But perhaps in the next vision, or another that will follow, you will see that I will come and embrace you in that time, and you will not be in the water alone."

The Master's comments about John's dream strike Iliam with incredible force. Clasping his right hand into a fist, he strikes his chest, bowing his head, and begins a soft, steady stream of chants. He brings his hands together and moves them up and down before him. Then, resting them upon his forehead, he bows unto Jesus. "Thou art He. Thou art the Promise of God. For naught but I know of this vision of John standing alone in the water, save those who were with him in the vision. And Thou hast said it. Thou wert with him in spirit as Thou art now with us all in body."

Jesus simply smiles and nods at Iliam.

Daniel and the other adepts are illumined by this demonstration that clearly this truly is the Chosen One.

"Good enough," John responds. "Thank you, my Brother. Thank you, Iliam. Thank you all for your patience."

Jesus begins to laugh. He clasps John's hand heartily and yanks him. John falls on the Master and they roll down the slight incline, laughing and jostling one another.

All the young adepts applaud and laugh, for it is a sight they have seen often with these two and, indeed, among themselves occasionally. Finally, John and the Master arise and stride, arms on one another's shoulder, then seat themselves, speaking softly, still laughing.

The adepts are struck by the obvious demonstration of the power of this young One and the unquestioning faith of the one called John.

A hand comes up again and Moira laughs lightly as Iliam points to her.

"Yes, Moira, please. Let us hear your question now."

Moira stands and straightens her garments, folding her hands in front of herself. As is oft her custom, she rocks from side to side just a bit as she speaks. "I, too, had a vision from God, and in it I saw something like my brother John's, but different. I felt a river of something, but it was not water. It was made up of colored winds or something. You know how after the storms, God presents the beautiful colors arching across the sky as the symbol of His Promise to our people?"

All nod.

"It was like that. The colors were vibrant, beautiful, and I was riding along in them! I thought, *Moira, why not try gliding in the different colors.* So just as easily as this," she takes a large step to her left, "I moved from the center of the rainbow down into the yellow, and I felt the yellow going all through my body, like spring flowers. It made me feel so good. I felt light and alive, and an energy stimulated me all over.

"So then I said, *Moira, try another color,*" at which point she takes two steps to her right to demonstrate, "and I found myself in the most brilliant red. We were sailing along on this river of red wind and, oh, it was glorious. Right here," she thumps her chest, "I felt this power of love, and I could hear singing somewhere way off. Sort of like you do." She points to a small group of adepts, the beauty of whose morning and evening ritual of song is admired by all.

The adepts smile and respond kindly to the acknowledgment of the power of the love in their song, their ceremony.

"So then I thought, *What about these other colors? What do they feel like?* So I went from one to the other to the other. Then I awoke. When I did, I felt like I was filled up to the top with all the colors." She turns to face her young brothers and sisters. "Can anyone see them in or around me yet?"

All of the group lean this way and that. Some shade their eyes from the early morning light, others look and blink.

Finally, one smiles, and then another, and another.

Iliam points to Jessie and asks, "What do you see?"

"Oh, I see such beautiful colors around you, right there."

Moira looks down and points to her heart. "Here?"

"Yes! Yellows, and above that some greens. And over here," she points to one side, "I see beautiful lavenders."

"Who else?" Iliam calls out.

"I see them," responds John.

"And I," adds the Master.

"I, too," James echoes.

"What seest thou, James?" questions Iliam.

"I do not see them quite as Jessie does. What I see is more like large circles of light swirling around her, each one in its own space, moving at its own speed, pulsing sort of like you can feel the body fluids pulse in your arm." He sticks out his arm and points to the crease at his elbow.

"What do you think that means, James?"

He rubs his face and chin. "I think it means she has been blessed. I think they are gifts from God, and I think they are well deserved, for she is a vessel worthy of carrying such beautiful gifts from Him."

Moira's face flushes. She looks down and then glances back up, for she has a deep and abiding love for James and considerable respect for his keenness of sight.

"Thank you, sweet Moira. Any others?"

So it continues. Many hands go up and questions are asked and answered. Each time, several of the adepts move close to those who question, as though to give them some sort of unseen blessing or energy.

Finally Daniel rises, and there is a hush. "Do you remember the teaching about the laws?"

Some scratch their heads, others look up and about, as they ponder.

"Let me be more specific. It was at the Sacred Spring, when you were taught about why water flows from on high to the sea." All of the faces brighten with recognition. "You were taught that this is according to a certain law and that there are many such laws, or forces or principles as they are also called, that are constantly at work, constantly present in the Earth and, indeed, beyond it. This morning, my brothers and sisters and I would like to aid you in opening your consciousness even further, to give you greater empowerment by understanding more about these principles.

"So, now think of the stream and the Holy Spring that you are so familiar with as a reference point, then think of yourself as if you *are* that stream and that Spring."

Some turn this way and that to see if any of their brethren have grasped this. Many close their eyes and become still. Gentle smiles appear all around, indicating that introspective reflection is everywhere.

"Your spirit is like the Sacred Spring," Daniel continues. "It pours forth from a Source that may not be seen outwardly, but is unlimited, eternal. It requires naught from you in terms of effort to bring it forth, but the more you look for it and see it and claim it, the greater becomes its flow. Do you comprehend this, my brothers and sisters?"

They look around at each other. A hand comes up.

Daniel acknowledges him. "Yes, please."

"I understand in principle what you are saying, that this Holy Spring within us is our spirit. But I do not understand what we are to do with it, or how we are to use it. Could you help me?"

"You are Thomas, correct?"

"I am, good sir."

"The use of that which is within is why you are all here. In order to understand how one might use the power and beauty, the magnificence of the Eternal Flow within, one must first understand it outwardly. This shall be our work, our focus for today. If you will bear with me for a time, I will attempt to answer your question in a broad sense. And if that does not suffice, I humbly ask you to repeat your question a bit later. Agreed?"

"Very good," Thomas replies, smiling. Looking about, he reseats himself, straightening his garments as he does.

"Let us carry this thought a bit further," Daniel continues. "Consider that you live in a sea of such energy. It is just like the Sacred Spring that flows downward and becomes a part of the sea. To most who perceive it thereafter, its singularity is obscured, for many streams run into the sea and become as one. And all of the thoughts and activities that are a part of their journey and a part of the sea itself impart their own essence to it, whether we judge this good or bad. True?"

Heads bob in affirmation.

"As in the example that I gave, so it is with our spirits and the life force. This force flows into life itself through our thoughts, through all our words and deeds. What we feel and hold within flows from within us into the outer world."

"How does it do that?" questions Jessie.

"Ah! Now we approach an area that will truly be of some interest to all of you, I should think," Daniel responds. "You have studied the power of your thoughts and your emotions, what you hold in your heart." All nod. "You know the power of your prayers. Well, it is the same as this. What you hold within, even though you believe it to be only within you, you are sending forth just as surely as a spring that is continually flowing. In other words, your life force is as a spring of energy that flows into the sea of energy, which is life. Before you all raise your hands," he adds, recognizing that many are popping up all over, "let me explain further.

"Look about you. You see many of your brothers and sisters, and many who are adepts here at our sacred School. You see the land, the plants, the animals, the sky above. All of this is energy. Remember the teachings? Well, this energy flows from within you to the without, continuously."

"Have I no control over it?" questions Jessie.

Several of the others laugh softly.

"Indeed you do," Daniel replies, straightening himself. "That is the first point we wish to emphasize to you all. You have control over the life that you give to the sea of life. Remembering the Sacred Spring and how it flows, pure, nourishing, and unencumbered to join the Great Sea. If you choose to let your life force flow as an energy of life into the sea of life that is called the world …" he gestures, "if you do this," pointing to Jessie, "and you," pointing to Moira and others, "and you are like the purity of the Sacred Spring, only many-fold over, would not the sea become purer where you give to it?"

Jessie smiles. "I believe I understand. So, if I hold pure thoughts, if I hold joyful thoughts, whether I speak them or act them, just holding them within is what I am giving to the sea of life?"

"Yes," Daniel responds. "But first there is an important point we all wish to emphasize to you."

Thomas is becoming impatient. "What is it?" Many laugh aloud. He glances this way and that, smiling, but he turns back to Daniel, for the question is sincere.

"Simply that you must first take of it for yourself, before you can give it."

"What do you mean? If I have this beautiful stream of life flowing through me," Thomas rubs his torso, "which now I know I do, thank you, why would it not simply flow from me to the sea of life in that pure form in which it springs forth within me … from God, I assume, correct?"

Daniel smiles and nods.

"Well, then, what do you mean, I must take of it?"

"Because it runs through you." Daniel speaks slowly, for emphasis.

Thomas narrows his eyes, lifting his hand to his head and scratching it. "You mean more literally, we are like the stream. The Spring is the spirit within us and we are the channels through which it flows. So, if we do not take of it, do we somehow pollute it? Like what can happen to streams?"

"Very good. What comes from you must come from you totally, or it loses its effect. It loses its power."

"I have it," Thomas affirms softly. "I have it." He stands up. "I know what you are teaching us. You are telling us that to be instruments of that within, we must become like that which we seek to give, or else we pollute or diminish it. And if we can become as it is and truly take it for ourselves, then we know it and can give it, and that is our gift to the sea of life. Yes. I understand." He seats himself. "Thank you."

Many begin to clap for Thomas, who leans this way and that, exaggeratedly accepting their applause. Smiling, he straightens himself. "Thank you very much."

Daniel is studying Iliam as though to say, *Where to next, do you think?*

Iliam nods and turns to the group. "If you are out and about in life and you encounter a group of individuals and a place that is polluted with thoughts and emotions that cloud or block or limit the flow of the holy Spring within as you move into it, it has its natural effect. It is a part of what has been taught to you, our laws, that the greater number, the greater energy, is a more powerful challenge to you individually. How can you deal with this?"

Again, Thomas raises his hand, and Iliam nods. "It just means that I must go to the Spring within myself and redouble my efforts and claim more and more for myself, that I become impenetrable, impervious, to that which is without. Is that correct?"

"That is a good way, yes. Does anyone have another?"

"I think I do," James answers. "I would in such an instance recognize that I am not alone. Though I would appear to be alone, when I affirm within that I am not alone, but am with all of you at all times, merely recognizing and recalling that truth in those moments makes it so. Is that not true?"

Smiling, Iliam nods. "Then what would you do, James, once you have accomplished this?"

"I would immediately bring that into the midst of the polluted thought and emotion."

"Would you do anything else?" Iliam inquires gently.

"Yes, I would. I would hold it as a powerful thought. I would send it out as an emotion, as a gift of love and compassion, to all those about."

"And if they react adversely to you for doing so? Then what would you do?"

"I would do as my brother said." He gestures to Thomas. "I would go within and redouble my efforts. I would revisit each of you, accepting your gift of light and love, and I would make that so powerful that naught could penetrate it."

A prolonged silence falls.

"How would you answer this question?" inquires Daniel. "Which is the greater, for you to say the word *love* aloud or for you to say it within?"

There is another long pause as many contemplate this. One can actually see them considering it.

John raises his hand and is recognized. "I think that love is a power which has no limitation, that love is the power that can transcend all things. So your question is interesting, but has no merit, for if one has love powerfully enough within, it need not be spoken. It simply is."

At this, we see the Master smiling and nodding at John.

"What say you, Jesus, to your brother's comments?"

"I have naught to add to them, save this … In the Earth it is often helpful to those whom one meets to hear a thing spoken, for their internal sight and hearing are dimmed. And yet I agree utterly with my brother; God's Love, flowing through a vessel who has claimed it with the faith that he does need not be spoken. It is as he is, and therefore the word is not needed. But there are those times when I know that he will speak it, just as shall I, and all of you. And perhaps that is not because of what your question implies, but rather the needs of others who hear not, neither do they see."

John nods, affirming his realization that, yes, he can envision that there will be times when holding a thought, affirming the oneness of God's Love for self and all others, will need to be expressed in word and deed.

Without invitation the Master continues, "We perform ... our peoples and yours, for we are one ... an array of ceremonies and celebrations which we know to be holy. We cherish them because of the love and faith of our ancestors and because our sweet sisters and brothers in our homeland revere these expressions. So we, too, revere and perform them. For claiming actions as testimony, as gifts, and doing so severally rather than alone gives them greater power.

"I am told here," Jesus says, pointing to his heart, "that if I believe a thing to be so, then so is it." Without looking at him, He reaches His left arm out to place it upon John and His right arm to embrace Andrew. "But if we speak it, if we perform the same action together, the same ceremony with the same intent and faith, now it is borne unto the Earth. If he does it alone," turning to look at Andrew, "it is his. And if he does it alone," looking at John, "it is his. But if they and I do it together, it is born. It is. So, as we believe unto a thing and testify unto our belief, then it shall be."

He lowers His hands and arms from around His brothers and sits serenely gazing at Daniel and Iliam. "Of course, thou knowest these things, and so I give them that they might be spoken, that we shall know them together." Jesus turns to look around at His brothers and sisters. "The Kingdom of God truly is within us. And that which thou hast given us in thy teachings," He looks lovingly at Daniel and Iliam, "is as giving us the keys to open that Kingdom unto all of the world, that we might come unto any who are lost or who dwell in darkness, mindful of our heritage, mindful of our bond of oneness, and mindful that we, together, are birthing this.

"We can say unto that one who is lost, *Come ye here, unto me, for I am the Light and the Way*, and as we speak this, we speak it in one voice. Whether that voice comes through me or through any of you, my brothers and sisters, it is in that moment being spoken by all our spirits. No longer the many beautiful streams of spirit flowing through each of us individually, but as one mighty river of Light flowing from God because we have chosen it to be.

"Then your vision of the river of many colors, sweet Moira, takes on new meaning. For each color is likened unto each of us, a beautiful aspect of God, wondrously rich with gifts to be given. Individually, we might be noted only in passing. But together we are the rainbow of God, His heavenly promise coming from above and descending upon the Earth, showering it with the gifts we bear in His Name."

Chapter Three

The Good Seed

he large chamber that lies beneath the great rugged crags of the School of the Prophets is brightly lit. Within it are all those Expectant Ones who have been received.

Leading the commentary at present is Elob who represents, figuratively and literally, the leadership of the adepts. "Some of you, dear brothers and sisters, will depart soon. Prior to your departure there will be the preparation, to be thought of in some respects as the closing of these works and this portion of your life until now. As part of that closure, certain gifts will be given to empower you to meet that which lies ahead. Those of you who depart will travel into diverse locations in the outer world where you shall dwell and become one with those who dwell there, learning to understand their thoughts, their attitudes, the structure of their societies and much more. At a future time, some of you will be called, and when you are, that which has been placed to rest within you will be reawakened. You will know Him, for He will speak these words to you: *Follow me.*

"In all that has been offered to you, you have discovered many great gifts within. No matter how these are placed within you, nor that which is a part of the process of placing them at rest, they shall be as many beautiful lights awaiting any need to be called forth and awaiting that time when they shall be reassembled, at which point your awakening shall contribute unto the work which will then follow."

Elob turns and glances around the sizeable group. "Those of you who will remain will be chosen according to that which guides you within, whereupon various paths will be offered to you. From these, your spirit will guide, and we shall nurture that guidance to bring it to its fruition.

"The bond of light that has formed between all of us in these joyous activities during your tenure here is an eternal one. We shall look in upon you in vision and meditation, and offer our prayers as we do. On behalf of all my brothers and sisters, we give our thanks to you for the gifts you have given to us and pray only that those we have shared with you serve you well."

So the conversation continues, culminating in questions from the group.

As the evening's activities draw to a close, the Essenes move into groups, guided if not led by, various adepts from the School.

Those who are to remain move into the night, up a slope and over to where the grand concourse is located. Seated around the large campfire are many of the School's adepts, among whom the arriving group intersperse themselves. The conversation begins again, among two or three here, several over there, and so forth.

Those who are to depart are taken to a secondary chamber where they are given many suggestions about how to use that which they know in the life to which they are embarking. Throughout the evening they are called, one by one.

Here, one such is seated before two of the adepts. Small oil lamps burn intermittently, one of which is positioned between the Essene and the adepts.

"Close your eyes now," begins the first adept, "and listen carefully, releasing all thought and holding the image of this place as you look upon it in your consciousness."

The second adept begins to chant quietly in a mesmerizing voice.

Soon, the first adept speaks again, slowly, in a hypnotic tone that seems to undulate like the repetition of gentle waves upon a seashore. "All that you have learned is within you and shall be at rest. You shall open your mind, your consciousness, and your senses, to that which lies ahead. You shall be able to call upon that within you whensoever there is a need. But until you are called forth, all these teachings and truths shall lie within you as a great light, strengthening you, giving unto your needs in every wise."

The chanting and the commentary continue but for a few brief moments. Upon concluding, the first adept reaches over to place his hand upon the forehead of the Essene. "In the Name of the One God may His peace surround and guide you. Let my words now become one with you. When I remove my hand you shall return to the flame before you, and all of my words shall then become one with your being."

With only several moments' pause, the first adept removes his hand from the Essene's forehead.

Timothy blinks several times, looks around, then smiling in recognition of the two adepts, says softly, "I heard all of your words clearly, and in hearing them, I found a part of myself asking how it could be possible that I would ever forget the beauty, the magnificence of all that has been."

The first adept smiles, glancing at the second, who then speaks. "You shall not forget it, or us. But what will happen after you sleep this evening is that upon awakening, you will gradually begin to shift your focus. As you journey back to your homeland and to what lies beyond, these works will begin to manifest, and their effect will take place gradually. That is by our design, and is to preserve and protect you, even though you know not why. Bless you, Timothy, and the work that lies ahead for you. We are ever one and with you."

The adepts rise first, then Timothy. Another adept comes and leads him out of the chamber.

Shortly, another adept brings a second Essene and seats him before the two adepts, and the process begins anew. This continues until all who are to depart have been blessed and guided, that the truth within them will be preserved and that their outer selves will function fully in dealing with the experiences that lie ahead, the calling that beckons each one.

He stirs the porridge thoughtfully, reaching to add a bit of honey to it, then grasps the cup of tea nearby, sipping it slowly, his eyes adjusting to the early morning light. He looks about pondering what lies ahead, reflecting upon the ceremony that has been completed for the departure of so many of his beloved brothers and sisters.

His mind drifts as he peers down into the flames before him. Suddenly the silence is broken by gasps in the group as a shrill sound comes from far off. John looks with concern at the Master, who is listening intently and gazing off into the dark passageway that leads to the wilderness beyond.

Again the call comes, followed by deep guttural coughs, and yet again.

Finally, John places the bowl on the ground beside him and, standing, looks down at the Master who is still gazing into the darkness.

But it is Iliam who addresses John. "It is undoubtedly a lion," he explains, looking up at John, who is now pacing back and forth.

"Well, whatever it is, it is asking for help. Do you not agree?"

"Indeed," Iliam acknowledges quietly.

"Jesus, let us go and see. Let us answer this call."

Looking up and smiling, Jesus says naught, but rises to His feet. Over to His right, several of their other brothers also rise, as does Iliam.

"I think not," he counsels the many who are prepared to answer this call with John and Jesus. "Your intent is good and

I ask blessings for you because of it, but this is a matter for only a few. If the event is as I anticipate, there will be some reaction on the part of the species, for we are foreign and to be feared. He points as he speaks the names, "Just you, Jesus, John ... and you, Moira."

Moira looks down, embarrassed. "I?"

"If it pleases you to serve with them."

"I would be ever pleased to serve with Jesus ... I mean, and John, of course," she adds flushing.

"Quickly, then, for that calling indicates a weakening." Iliam strides over to Elob and several of the other adepts. He looks at them briefly and receives an affirmation.

Elob rises and hands him two great skins of water. "I believe you will need these."

Iliam nods and places a hand upon Elob's shoulder in a gesture of brotherhood and silent communication.

Turning to glance at the three behind him, Iliam looks forward and strides into the passageway and the waiting darkness. Jesus, John, and Moira quickly follow, scurrying to keep up with Iliam's long, ground-covering strides. The silence of the early morn is broken only by the crunching of their footsteps against the earth beneath them.

On and on they move, beyond the rocky structure of the School, out into the wasteland dotted with rolling dune-like formations and sparsely located spiny plants, dimly visible in the pre-dawn light.

Finally, Iliam raises his hand. They stop.

A low, whining moan can be heard from just over the next rise.

Slipping the cord from one of the water skins on his shoulder, Iliam turns and hands it to John. Looking at Jesus, he blinks several times. Jesus' eyes fix upon him and soften, and an almost imperceptible nod passes between them.

Jesus slowly makes His way up over the rise, John to one side, Moira to the other, Iliam behind.

There, in the little sandy hollow, lies a great lioness, barely moving. Normally she would react powerfully at this point, but she has only enough strength left to raise her head, her half-open eyes glaring at them in defiance. Her right paw struggles to rise and finally falls back to the earth.

With a few short strides, Jesus stands a pace or two away from her. Her eyes have closed now and all that can be heard is her panting.

"She is at birth," Jesus explains to John and Moira.

"Oh-h," Moira moans softly. "Her life is fading. See? Look you around her."

"Yes, it is indeed fading," Jesus agrees.

"Here, let me through."

Moira gasps. "Have you no fear, John, no concern?"

"Why should I? He's here." He turns to smile and gesture at the Master.

Jesus chuckles softly. "Some aspects of God's Spirit are not fully acquainted with others," He offers looking down at the lioness, "but perhaps the call is to us, and perhaps this one knows that we mean it only well. Proceed, my brother. I shall, as you have asked, surround you both with prayer."

"And I as well," Moira adds.

As though this were no more than one of his brothers or sisters, John walks gently forward, kneels, and begins to stroke the great head of the beast.

An eye flickers and a low guttural sound begins to come forth. Again the right paw twitches as though the intent is to strike out, but there is no strength.

He continues stroking and murmuring indistinguishable words and sounds which, perhaps, are rising up from some strange wellspring within this one called John.

Slowly, gently, he lifts the great head that it is at a sufficient angle to receive a bit of water. He works from the water skin, slowly taking the hem of his garment, moistening it, and dabbing it here and there upon the great beast's head. Again and again he gives her water. The beast's mouth reacts. The great tongue comes forth, and with it a sound that is curiously almost like one of the mantras of the adepts. On and on John repeats the process.

At last, he slowly lowers her head, having removed his outer garment and positioned it to lie beneath the lion's head. Touching her all the while, he moves around behind her, running his hand up and down her back, on her spine.

Examining her, he whispers, "I must help. She is bound."

"Then do so," Jesus encourages him softly. Eyes shining, He adds, "Do what must be done."

Carefully, John reaches his hand within her and, finding the cub, strives to turn it, massaging it. The hindquarters of the beast stiffen, but, oddly, she seems to sense his intent. Again and again he struggles, pushing, moving, perspiration beading upon his forehead, his face tight, his eyes narrowed.

Finally, he pulls forth a cub. "Moira, come." She hurries over, falling to her knees, takes the cub and begins to wipe away the residue. "Give it life, Moira. Give it life!"

Blinking and looking from John to Jesus, she places the cub before her and begins to work its chest. Then, cupping her hand over its mouth, she bends and puts her mouth upon her hand and begins to blow, pushing, blowing.

Finally, the cub coughs and sputters.

"Again, Moira. Again," John urges as he continues to work with the mother.

And as she does so, the cub's feet begin to move in all directions at once, it seems, and Moira starts to giggle.

But John pays no heed. His hand is back in the womb of the great beast. "Here is another, Moira."

Now Jesus begins to chuckle, bending to accept the first cub from Moira as she reaches out to take the second.

Having seated Himself upon the opposite bank of the small hollow, Jesus strokes the first cub, speaking to it softly.

"Oh," Moira exclaims. "Look! This one is so cute."

John glances at her, shakes his head to and fro, and smiles for the first time in some moments. "What think you, my Brother? Is it complete?"

Jesus smiles broadly and shrugs His shoulders. "You are the midwife, John. I do not know if another is in there."

John laughs quietly. Clearly, the intensity of these moments has softened considerably.

"Are there not usually only two?" Moira asks.

"Well, I am not very experienced with these particular beasties," John answers with playful sarcasm, followed by a great smile, "but I suppose, if she will allow me, I can check."

The lioness is now breathing much more regularly.

"Oh my," John announces softly, "she has three." He pulls a smaller, final cub from the womb, stroking it, looking down at it.

"How is it?" the Master asks.

"Not well, it appears." His eyes fix upon the Master's.

Jesus nods, rises, and walks over to John. "Very well, certainly this is a creation of God. Here, take this one."

John takes the first cub in one arm and hands Jesus the third, smaller one. The Master turns and walks back to His previous position and seats Himself, wiping off the cub with His outer garment.

Moira and John are riveted, wondering what He will do, ever mindful of His oneness with God and the miracle that passed through Him to their brother, Justus.

Jesus cradles the third cub and, looking up, closes His eyes. A beautifully serene smile surfaces, and we hear soft words: "My Father, as Thou seest us here, look now upon this small one. I, Jesus, ask of Ye … Give it life. Bring it forth into the beauty of Thy creation. Let me be Thy instrument. As Thou hast blessed my brother John and sister Moira, so now bless me in Thy service."

He lowers His head to look upon the small cub, stroking it, drying it. After some coughing and expulsion of fluids and mucous, the cub stretches out one leg to place its tiny paw against Jesus' upper arm. Now the paw begins to knead, back and forth. The eyes blink and look up at Jesus and we hear low, guttural purring. "Thank You, Father. She is beautiful."

For a while, they continue to tend the cubs.

John returns periodically to rehydrate the mother. She lies kneading the Earth, looking at him with a curious emptiness in her eyes. He reaches to stroke her great head, and the lioness opens her mouth.

Moira gasps for a moment, but then smiles as she sees the tongue come out to brush against John's forearm. "Oh, look, John. She likes you."

"Well, I should think she likes all of us."

"No, it is different with you. Look at her."

As John watches her eyes softening, Moira notices that Jesus is staring up beyond, on the rise, and turns to look where He is staring. She gasps aloud once again as she sees the outline of a great mane. Sprawled out upon the top of a nearby ridge is an enormous male lion. "Uh-oh! I hope he knows we mean well."

"He does," Jesus assures her. "He has been watching all this time, I am sure."

"Do you think he will come here?"

"No," Jesus answers softly. "He is as our guardian priests who watch over all of us, I suspect."

"Look!" Moira gleefully holds up a little cub. "Look at your child." She laughs, cuddling the cub, which is now making curious oral sounds. "Oh, you are hungry. What do you think, John?"

"Bring her over, and the others, too."

Soon, as they stand looking down, they see the mother licking, grooming her new babies, as they knead her, suckling joyfully.

Having left nourishment as best they have to give, Jesus, John, and Moira turn and begin to stride away.

Iliam is standing below, smiling, almost forgotten. "All is well, then?"

"Oh, yes," Moira exclaims. "Why did you not come? You should have seen it. It was beautiful."

"Well, I believe that the three of you have made some dear friends. And, who knows? A time may come when they will return your gifts and watch over you, as you have cared for them. Who can say?"

Jesus is smiling, for He has seen a time ahead of journeys into the wilderness, and He knows that quite possibly, if not likely, they shall meet these creatures of God again. When they do, the warmth and love of their hearts will be remembered and returned. Jesus turns to look at John, for He knows that he will be blessed aplenty from the harvest of the good seed sown this day.

"What happened?" questions one of the others, as they rejoin the group.

Moira excitedly begins to relate the story, elaborating all the details, taking great care in describing each of them, as one whose joy cannot be contained.

Finally, John begins to laugh, "Oh, Moira! I believe you are well qualified to be a scribe. Such detail even I did not note, and I was there."

Jesus laughs and throws an arm around him, embracing him mightily.

"It is important for you all to look upon this scene and to know it utterly," Iliam begins. "Go out and move about, touch or sit on any of the rocks, whatever you must do to know this particular location completely."

Some time passes as the young Essenes do so … touching, feeling, sitting, scooping up some earth to look at it, even rubbing sumptuous handfuls of sand between their palms.

Finally, a few adepts who have been standing with Iliam come forward and, under the direction of one of them, Marta, they spread small shawls on the ground. Each of these has a unique pattern. Quite lovely colors are woven intermittently, and their patterns are strong, vibrant. "I am called Marta. Look upon these shawls now before you. They are seating shawls and each of you shall have one. The symbols you see on them all have been placed there under the direction of Rebochien."

"Rebochien?" questions James curiously. "Our teacher?"

"Yes, he directed our weaving. The pattern he discerned for each of you is depicted in the weaving. Come you, each, and find that which is yours."

James looks across at Phillip who shrugs his shoulders and smiles, as though to say, *I am not quite sure how I will know mine, but I imagine trusting the process is what is required.*

Knowing each other's thoughts, James extends a hand to Phillip and they walk in kinship, hand in hand among the shawls.

All the others are walking about, too, some commenting about the beauty of a particular design or a unique color.

Moira and Jessie survey them all in wonder.

Oh, Jessie, the colors are so vibrant!

"I have not seen such colors, for our peoples do not have them."

"They are colors from the east."

"Do you think you have found your shawl?" asks Jessie.

"I believe so," Moira bends down to study a particular shawl. Circular swirls begin in one corner and curiously intertwine to arrive at the center where the color is brighter, yet of a delicate rose. Then a pink line or channel of color seems to move away and intertwine with the first one to move to the upper right corner, as though the color were flowing out of it.

Marta is noting this and comes to Moira's side. "Tell me what you see."

Moira falls to her knees to point at the shawl. "See here? This is where I entered. This is the path of my life through the present, here, in the center." She places her hand upon the beautiful rose color, her eyes flickering, a warm smile lighting her face. "I feel it. I feel me in the pattern. And here I am, right now. It is like my heart is here."

"And the path which leaves … What say you of that?" Marta is obviously pleased.

"It is what I have to give. See? Here, I have come in spirit, and here I am in consciousness at the center, and this is my intent, my gift to the world. It flows from me as my spirit is drawing its resources from God."

"Unquestionably, sweet sister, this is your shawl. Sit upon it, if you will."

Brushing it gently, Moira sits down carefully, crosses her legs, straightens her garment, and assumes a position of prayerful meditation.

Glancing over to the side, Marta walks a few paces away to where Jessie has stopped and is running her hands over a shawl. "Is this not beautiful? See here. Look at the lovely, vibrant greens. It makes joy spring into my heart. And look over here where the soft blues radiate from the four corners of the shawl to the center, and then intermingle. And look you here, how the center gives back to the four corners. It is just as we do when we receive from and give to the four great power points in the world."

Marta smiles at Jessie. "Claim the shawl, then, for it has obviously claimed you."

So Jessie, as well, positions herself with great care, straightening the corners and edges of the shawl as she does.

All of them now have found their own special gift, and they are sitting upon them. Time passes as the adepts allow them to exchange comments and *oo-os* and *ah-hs* about the uniqueness of one another's shawl and to meditate and pray.

Then Elob addresses them. "Gather up your shawls, now,

and come with me."

He leads them to the great chamber wherein not that long ago they said farewell to many of their brothers and sisters. Its size seems doubled because their number is so much fewer. Guided under the watchful eye of many of the adepts of the School, they position themselves upon their shawls, arranged in a generous circle. Behind each Essene stand at least two adepts.

Elob walks to the center of the group. "Welcome, brothers and sisters. What we shall do here is important for each of you in your journey ahead. The gift you have been given upon which you are now seated carries the love and truths of our brothers and sisters here in the School. It is our prayer that these shawls bring to you the intent that is woven into them. You have all reached a point through these many months of study with us here, and the years that went before among your own beautiful peoples, where now I should like to call you *candidates*. The accomplishment to which you are now to be guided is the recognition, awakening, and claiming of your own oneness.

"Some of you will go beyond our School to a work that is important to your uniqueness as individuals as well as to the Promise, of which you are an integral part. The rest of you should not look at this as any form of evaluation. Such a path of self-judgment may call to you, but I know your hearts and spirits are clear and strong, and I know you will not answer that call but will stay aright upon the path of truth.

"Each of you has a brother or sister from our School who shall become your mentors, your guides. They are the ones who have assisted in the weaving of your shawl. They are the ones who hold you, personally (as well as all of you, of course) … but you individually and personally in a special place in their hearts and prayers. They have chosen you by the guidance of God. All of them have been upon a fast and prayer vigil for three days and nights. And God, so they have seen it, has pointed to you, and given you to them as their gift of service. Mind you, they are no greater nor lesser than you or any of us. For the first veil of their sight of truth is equality. Each of them sees through this and can know what lies beyond because the veil of truth opens, not closes, makes clear, rather than clouds as veils of the Earth might do.

"This veil of truth is a step along the path that shall culminate for some of you, as I have said, in the Great Initiation. For others of you it will lead to a great role of service to people in the outer world, and to the Promise to be fulfilled in a far-distant time.

"Now, as your mentors assist you, you will reawaken the memory of the location with which you were earlier asked to become familiar. Do this now, with their assistance."

Each of the Essenes, now called candidates, exchanges comments with their mentors, little suggestions for various adjustments. Over here, one mentor begins to gently rub Thomas around the neck and shoulders, helping him to raise the energy, so to say, because of a momentary blockage. Over there, another adjusts Philip's garments around the upper shoulder area so he will not be distracted, explaining all the while the reasons for doing this. On and on it goes.

"In a moment," Elob continues, standing in the center, "there will be no light within this sacred chamber. In the area outside with which you have become one, others of our brothers and sisters are watching … They are observing, looking for your appearance there."

As Elob raises his hands, the adepts move to extinguish the oil lamps here, there, until only one remains at Elob's feet, casting curious, mystical dances of light upon the faces and bodies of the candidates. Elob slowly walks around that small lamp as he quietly gives instructions. "Straighten yourselves. Let your thought rise from the Earth to beyond. Feel your consciousness as it dwells at the top of your being. Recall the image of the location that you have become one with. I shall speak three names aloud. You will not understand them, for they are in my native tongue. Upon hearing the third, become one with the vision, the memory, and *be* there. You will do this by bringing the consciousness of your being upwards. Draw in a breath and bring it to the fullness of the crown of your being. And when you exhale that breath, send yourself forth to be in that locale with which you have become one."

He speaks the first name, and silence follows. He speaks the second name. Again, silence.

The third name comes as though the heavens have opened and a great bolt of lightning passes through the consciousness of the candidates. Some gasp, some moan in delight and wonder.

In the target location, beyond the chamber, the adepts point here, there ... Shimmering forms are congealing around them, one upon a rock over here, another standing, turning about over there.

"Come forth," one of the adepts calls out strongly, "Come, we receive you. Come. Let your thought be free. You are eternal. You are spirit. The body is as clothing. Set the clothing aside, and be with us."

These words and thought-forms seem to empower the group within the chamber.

A number of the adepts in the outer location are seated, rocking to and fro, chanting, offering prayers. Singsong lyrics fill the gentle slopes on either side. The candidates are forming. Some are strikingly visible. They look at one another.

Finally, the adept spokesperson in the chamber raises her hands and claps them strongly, briskly, above her head. The sound seems to have a rippling energic effect upon the shimmering forms. One by one they dissipate and are gone from the target location.

"Bring light," Elob requests quietly.

From the long passageway that twists and turns to the outside, light can be perceived from the absolute darkness in the great chamber. Slowly, the lamps are illuminated.

Some of the candidates are chattering, laughing.

"I did it!" Phillip exclaims softly, in amazement. He looks over at James on his right. "Did you see me?"

"I did! Clearly. And I could not have seen you had I not also been there!" The two laugh and chatter excitedly.

Across from them, Jesus, Moira, Nathanael, and a number of others are seated quietly.

Jesus is smiling calmly, His hands resting upon His knees. Looking at His countenance, one would assume that this entire matter is of no great consequence to Him.

Elob has noted this. "What say you, Jesus?"

"In regard to what?" Jesus smiles playfully.

"In regard to this experience on the part of your brothers and sisters."

Jesus leans a little to look around the group. "Well, wait until next time. They will do so much better, it will be beyond belief."

Several chuckle a little, but Thomas remarks off to the side, "This was beyond belief, Jesus! You mean it gets better than this? I actually saw the adepts out there. I can tell you everything about them. It is almost more than my mind is capable of holding."

Jesus leans forward and places His chin upon one hand. "Why would that be, Thomas?"

"Well, you know … My physical body was not really out there. So I have to ask myself, *Thomas, what is it that did the seeing outside?* And I have a little trouble with that answer."

Jesus straightens up, smiling expansively at Thomas, who obviously pleases Him with his exploration of the details and mechanisms. "Remember, my brother, the more frequent the experience, the more real it becomes."

"Are you saying that we will do this frequently?"

Jesus lifts His hands and feigns a lack of knowledge. "Who can say? All I am doing is reminding you of that which you already know. And for that matter, that is all that life does. Would you not say?" He leans back and laughs.

"Once you know of pain, it has no further purpose for you," Marta is explaining, as she and other adepts guide the candidates in healing works. "Pain is only, you might call it, a messenger to tell you that some attention is needed."

"Then, why do some people prolong pain, if it is only needed to receive a message?" Jessie asks. "I can recall some years back when one of those … What did you call it?" She searches her mind for a memory. "Well, one of those stingy things struck me, right here." She moves her garment to show a place above her right ankle. "That pain did not go away for a long time. My sweet sister Hannah put a poultice on it, and Mary gave it God's Grace. But even with all that, it was some time before that pain went away completely."

"Can you remember why?"

"Why? Uh-h … You mean why the pain stayed?"

"Yes."

"Maybe because I paid attention to it. It was a very big thing, you know, to have one of those stingy things strike. We have been told that some who do not have our knowledge cross over the Bridge of Light when that happens! They are deadly little things."

"I should like to ask a question here, if I might."

"Marta nods. "Yes, Thomas?"

"Why is it that sometimes when we seek to do a healing work for one who has asked, that I have a difficult time finding my own spirit to bring it forth to serve … You know, as the vessel of God's healing grace. Why is that?"

Glancing around to look at all the candidates, Marta's eyes fall upon John. "John, bring forth your bowl, please."

John reaches within his garments and does so.

"Go, take that flask and fill your bowl with water."

Without questioning, John rises and walks over to the side. Lifting the flask, he fills his bowl with water and brings it back, kneeling and holding it up to Marta.

"What do you see in the bowl, Thomas?"

John turns to show the bowl to Thomas.

"Well, I see what is there, of course ... water."

"Bring forth your bowl, Thomas."

He reaches within his garment and pulls his own bowl forth, for each candidate carries their own sacred bowl.

"What is within your bowl?"

Thomas stares at Marta with obvious frustration. "Of course, there is nothing."

"Why do you believe that to be so?"

Thomas looks down and then back at her, lifting his bowl up and tipping it sideways. "That is why I believe it to be so." Then he brings the bowl back down.

The candidates all remain silent.

Marta looks across the circle. "Jesus, would you assist?"

He rises and strides over to kneel beside John, in front of Marta.

"Bring forth your bowl, if you would, please."

His eyes fixed upon Marta, Jesus knows what is about to come. He reaches within His garments, pulls forth His bowl, and holds it out.

"What does this bowl mean to you, Jesus?"

His eyes are still fixed upon Marta, a sweet smile on His face. "It means that I am expectant."

John has glanced at Jesus and looked down at His bowl.

"And knowing that this bowl symbolizes the Golden Cup within you, Jesus, how would you fill it, to answer a need and call before you, as Thomas has asked?"

His eyes still fixed upon Marta, Jesus answers quietly. "I would ask of my Father that if it be according to His Will, He fill this bowl that I might nourish another's needs from it."

"Do so."

Unblinking, Jesus gazes at her. His incredible aura of love and compassionate understanding fill the encampment. He closes His eyes. Holding the bowl in His right hand, He places His left over it and looks up. "Abba. Abba. Father, unto that which is a need before me, grant me Thy Spirit and the light thereof, as is sought by this one in need."

A melodic, tinkling sound becomes audible, though barely so, as John watches Jesus pass His hand back and forth, then away from the bowl, which is now filled with water.

In shock, Thomas looks down at his own empty bowl. John and Jesus study him. Recovering quickly, adeptly, as is his nature, Thomas questions Marta. "You say unto John, 'John, fill your bowl from yon flask,' so he did, and his bowl is full. You say unto Jesus, 'Jesus, fill this bowl with the spirit of the power of God within you,' and it is filled. How so is it that I, Thomas, might fill my bowl, for I am not the Promise, and you did not direct me to retrieve water from a flask? What means have I that will empower me to fill this bowl and claim my spirit within when one asks and is in need of healing?"

"John, empty thy bowl into Thomas'."

In one swift motion John so does.

"Fill thy bowl, John. Not from a flask, but from thy spirit within."

Hesitantly, John glances at Jesus, then over at Thomas and down at the water given by himself to Thomas. John feels a soft pressure on his right shoulder and turns to see the hand of Jesus upon it.

The Master's eyes are soft, rounded with love, and the pressure of His hand is an embrace, a touch of the very Spirit of God. Transfixed by this one beside him, John hears Jesus speak. "My brother, thou knowest the way. Thou knowest the Promise. The Spirit of God awaits your call to fill your bowl and your inner cup, that from these you might claim. Yea, verily I say to you that you might take away that which limits those who ask. That you might say the word, that the Spirit of God shall in Its time be upon the Earth. Say it, John, and thy bowl is filled, as is your inner cup."

The silence that follows is filled with the energies of John's faith being unleashed, of the love moving between all of these brothers and sisters, and of a brother who is seeking to claim.

In one graceful motion John's hand passes over his own bowl. He looks at it not, but lifts it up above him, slowly tilting it. All can see the water that pours forth.

Can you come unto the temple of your own wisdom and truth within, dear friends? Can you be placed in darkness and having memory of the light go unto it and be there? Can you question the Spirit of God and in so doing know It better and become one with It?

Perhaps you are that one who shall be called.

Perhaps you shall in a time not distant, but near, hear these words, and see the eyes of Him that speaketh them filled with love and compassion: Follow Me.

Chapter Four

Portal of Transition

Considerable time has elapsed … many months. The works and activities, the training and study, have intensified with the passage of each day. In the encampment this morning only a few Essenes and a few adepts from the School remain. The first rays of the sun's light are casting their golden fingers over the horizon's edge like a great beam of light shining on this select group.

It is Moira who notes it. She stands, shading her eyes from the dawn's light, and peers off in the distance, pointing to the desert. "What is that out there?"

Several adepts hurry to her side to look in the direction she is indicating, pondering initially, *Are we discovered? Are there, somehow, those who have found our Sacred School?*

Indeed, a small group of figures can be seen moving somewhat slowly across the space between the group's location and the great School.

Gesturing as he turns, one of the adepts scurries up to a higher point, that which is now called Reflection Rock in honor of the Forerunner's claim. "I can see them," the adept calls down. "And I see their staffs shining."

"Oh," Moira clutches her heart, "guardians! It must be."

She, Jessie, Bartholomew, and several others scramble to grab their over-garments and whisk them about their bodies, moving without hesitation down the slope and into the edge of the wilderness.

"Oh, Simeon!" Moira rushes over to embrace him. "And Bartholomew! I greet you in love and brotherhood."

Nathanael comes up from behind, his brow moist with perspiration.

As Moira glances beyond him and Simeon, she sees a litter and upon it a great figure resting quietly, unmoving. "What is this?" she inquires softly.

Nathanael answers with obvious reverence and love in his voice. "It is our brother, Gideon. We know not what is amiss. The Holy Sisters have done all they know to do and so have all the others, yet he still sleeps. We fear soon he will have naught to sustain his body, and so we have brought him here, begging humbly that our Lord might call him forth."

The assembly quickly brings Gideon and the others to the encampment up within the School's confines. Its great craggy outcroppings and majestic sculpted figures present an awe-inspiring sight.

"Who are the others back there?"

At this, Nathanael smiles broadly. "That is a surprise, Moira, and you will see soon enough. But, might we tend to Gideon? Would you call Jesus, please?"

Moira glances down at Jessie and Bartholomew, who are stroking Gideon's brow with a moist cloth, then back up. "He and many of the others are not here, Nathanael. They are off to the Great Library."

Nathanael lowers his eyes. He known this means that they are a considerable distance away, and that even if Jesus were to be called to return, by the time one could travel to Alexandria and back, it is likely that his dear brother, the warrior priest called Gideon, would be no more in this world. Looking up, Nathanael's eyes are soft. "Are there those of the School, or perhaps some of you who have learned as the Master has, and could do the work?"

Moira stiffens and reaches out to clasp Jessie's hand.

Bartholomew glances up just for a moment and then lowers his gaze to continue his tender care of Gideon.

A goodly number of the adepts close at hand speak softly among themselves. One comes forward. "We will dispatch one of our brothers and a company to ask that Jesus and those with Him return. Until then, I and my brothers and sisters have the power to sustain him."

Two of them step forth. Bartholomew moves aside, and they kneel before Gideon. One has prepared a bowl of special herbs, and tenderly lifting Gideon's head he carefully places a few drops at a time into Gideon's mouth, massaging his face, shoulders, and chest. The other has placed her hands on his torso and lifts her face upwards, her eyes closed. After a time she looks at Nathanael. "Yes, we have the herbs to balance these errant energies. He has been poisoned by something."

Nathanael glances quickly over to Simeon, who shakes his head. "We know not how this could come to be."

"It matters not," the adept replies. "We here at the School know of such things. We can stop the progression of this toxin and sustain him at this point so he will progress no further unto the doorway of the great light beyond." Looking over towards the passageway, she nods to several of her brethren who are preparing to depart. They have water skins over their shoulders, staffs, and all else needed.

They gesture a symbol of oneness to her.

She nods in reply, indicating for them to depart.

Jesus is strolling casually among the great scrolls and the places that are set aside for those interested in studying them.

James and a number of the others are sitting off to the side at a table, carefully going over one of these scrolls. Iliam and Elob are speaking with him and several of the others, as they review what is recorded therein.

"This is incredible. What is the nature of the people who have recorded this?"

"Some say, James, that they are timeless, and beyond the measure of our understanding of age. They are called the Ancient Ones of Atlan."

"Where is this place, Atlan? I would visit it," he responds quickly, with excitement.

"It is naught, we fear," Iliam responds, "save for perhaps some remnants said to be in the interior, to the south."

"How far would you surmise that to be?"

"We know not. It is only told as a legend. Some say it is not true. Others swear it is."

James returns to studying the scroll, struggling with its languages and symbols, yet he feels a oneness with it. Hands caressing the parchment, he unrolls it as though it were something that was literally a part of him.

Elob now draws Iliam off to the side, speaking quietly. "No question. Look at him, look at the energy around him."

Nodding as he gazes at James from a distance, Iliam turns back to Elob. "He has been one of them, no doubt."

Jesus continues to casually walk about, hands clasped behind Him, not retrieving a single volume or scroll, but simply looking, perusing. He notices the many diversified entities present, pondering their curious garb and the differences in their facial structure, and He feels a growing light within Himself. For He senses in a time not distant, but near, that He will be in the energies of those lands, the womb of which has brought these peoples forth.

"From whence comest thou?" Jesus speaks softly, but with authority.

The three to whom this question is obviously addressed turn quickly and glance at one another. "Who art thou that asks this of us?" one demands.

"I am but a simple traveler. I am come from the uplands, a carpenter."

"We are from the lands far to the east, where the crescent and star come to oneness. We are followers of that sacred truth that has led us here, and are seeking the writings of those of our peoples who have gone before. As our great teachers have told us, emissaries many hundreds of years ago brought the scrolls here to this great Library of Knowledge so our peoples and our faith might be known."

Nodding and smiling just a bit, Jesus responds quietly. "That is very honorable, and it is good that your peoples and their ways, and you as a part of those, seek to uphold this. For one is known by that which has gone before. And the words of those who have gone before are the seeds which bring to harvest that which is in this day and the days ahead."

The eyebrows arch upon two of the travelers, as they look at one another. "Who art thou to speak such words?" asks the taller one in the center.

"I am called Jesus."

There is a long pause. "We are of some knowledge of your name. Thou art that one from the Holy Ones."

"I am He."

After they confer in a small huddle, silently glancing over at Him, one asks, "Knowest thou of our teachers?"

"I do."

"Have you the evidence of this knowledge?"

Without a word Jesus smiles and makes the gesture He has seen so oft from those at the School, whom He so loves.

They gasp, break into great smiles, and move quickly over to Him, taking His hands, touching His shoulders. "We are come to find you."

"Why would John not come the last distance with us?" Iliam asks gently.

Elob shakes his head. "It is something within him, I suppose. I feel no right to intrude, to question it. To look upon him and to see in his eyes such a will, such determination, not I shall question it!" Elob smiles. "For he must follow the light and guidance within."

"Yes, of course. But heretofore," Iliam glances at Jesus, deep in conversation with the three strangers from the east, "they have been almost inseparable, except when one or the other or both of them have gone off to fast and pray … very often, I might add." Iliam laughs softly. "So why now, at this momentous event, would John decline? And where is he?"

"You know him as well as I … better, in some respects."

Iliam is surprised at this, for Elob has known them all much longer.

"It is not the duration," Elob answers the unspoken question. "It is the connection with spirit, heart, mind. And your connection with them has been a complete one, hence, my words. Why do you ask these things? Have you a concern?"

Iliam, his eyes riveted on Elob's, knows that to speak other than truth would be pointless, for this, his great teacher, would know instantly.

"Aha!" Elob responds before Iliam can answer, "You have illuminated a place in your heart for him, have you not?"

Iliam is beaming. "That I have. Something about him calls to me. And even now, just to think of him and speak of him, I feel a sense of longing and … Well, I think you know."

They are completing preparations for their evening's meal at the camp that, by their reckoning, is sufficiently removed from the great Library for them to be safe.

Phillip, who has just returned from gathering herbs and such from the lands about, talks quietly with Stefan, who has returned from the other direction with an abundant supply of roots and seeds that he has gathered. So much so, that he lists to the side as he walks, laughing and remarking on the great bounty that is present in the Spirit of God called nature.

Suddenly, Phillip turns and points. "Look you, travelers coming! And rapidly! As best I can perceive, they are some of our brothers from the School."

Stefan drops his bundle of foodstuffs and cants his head

forward, straining to see in the dimming light. "Come! We must tell the others. Something is amiss. I can feel it."

They quickly describe what they have discerned to Elob and Iliam.

Jesus is seated, looking down at the flames of the evening fire. His hands are folded and, occasionally, His eyes close and open. He is rocking, almost imperceptibly. In the silence of eternity we hear these words, *Oh, Father. Speak unto me. It is I, Your son, and I seek of You guidance here. There cometh forth a need and a call from one whose love is great, whose embrace has kept me unto this day. Is it righteous, Father, that I answer this call I know they shall ask of me?* In the silence of eternity, we hear naught, but as we look upon the face of the Master we see a sense of peace and receptivity.

His eyes open and His face breaks into a smile. He rises swiftly in a fluid motion and steps a few paces over to where Iliam, Elob, and the brothers from the School are gathered, speaking about the situation.

"I will go," He says softly, to the surprise of all gathered.

Elob's face relaxes as he realizes immediately that, of course, He would know. "Let us take food unto our bodies and sing our songs and pray our prayers. Let us celebrate our oneness with God and each other, and rest for a time. Then, let us travel in the dark so no one can perceive us. Come, brothers, let us give thanks for the food we are about to eat and offer a prayer for that which lies ahead."

It is one of those evenings that at first is so filled with darkness that one questions the wisdom of walking even a few feet, especially through the wilderness. As some of the stars begin to cast their subtle light upon the shadowy darkness of the rolling terrain, it is as though the appearance of the light has called forth creatures of the night. Occasionally, one can hear the wings of one of these soaring past, searching unto its needs. Distant sounds stimulate a reaction in the hearer's body, as though the animal has taken up residence therein, and the sound of its call activates a mysterious center of energy that rushes, tingling, up and down the spine. Some in the group glance at one another, a few with some concern, for the sounds are powerful, mysterious, even foreboding.

The light of the stars has become steadily brighter. As the group comes over a small rise, the adept at the forefront quickly raises his hand, signaling all to stop. Barely perceptible, off in the distance upon a summit, a solitary figure can be seen seated cross-legged, head bowed.

As Jesus and James approach the rise to see what is amiss, Jesus peers into the semi-darkness and then begins to laugh. Without a word, He begins His long, steady strides, building to a trot.

The others look at one another, but His figure becomes smaller as He moves with remarkable rapidity across the land.

Suddenly, they see the figure on the distant knoll rise to his feet and the two figures rush towards one another.

Elob begins to laugh, and Iliam as well. "It has to be John," Iliam surmises, chuckling in amazement. Soon the group reaches the two and comes upon them arm in arm, laughing, chattering like childhood playmates might.

"Greetings," exclaims John brightly.

"Goodness, John, what art thou about, perched upon such a rise, here in the midst of the wilderness, in the dark of night?"

Feigning some lack of understanding, John glances all about and then fixing his eyes upon the group, comments with laughter in his voice, "Dark of night? I see no darkness, Iliam. All is visible, if one opens their sight."

Jesus throws His head back, laughing appreciatively. With His hand resting across John's shoulder, He rubs it.

They all seat themselves for a time, but prepare no fire for that might be seen from a great distance in this wilderness.

Having heard them tell of what is amiss, John jumps to his feet first and smiles forthrightly at Jesus. "Let us be about the journey! Our brother is in need, and you, my Brother, have the medicine unto that need."

Jesus simply nods, and they begin to move quickly.

They continue to stroke Gideon's brow. They flex and massage his limbs as well, arms and hands, legs and feet. Repeatedly, the two adepts also dispense drops of medicinal herbs into his mouth.

"I must say, he looks better."

The adepts glance up at Simeon, acknowledging this with smiles.

They make no attempt to muffle the sound of their coming. There is no need to do so, for no one who is not intended to knows of the School.

Stefan and Phillip go immediately to Gideon and, speaking in hushed tones with Bartholomew, kneel and begin to pray. Each of them touches Gideon differently, as though to impart what they individually have to give.

"Bring him here," Jesus directs softly. He gestures to a place with which all of the candidates have had considerable experience. "Over here."

Many of the other adepts have now gathered, forming a loose circle around the group. Across the earth, which has been carefully cleared of even the smallest pebble, a large robe has been spread and another, and another, until a thick blanket insulates Gideon from any irritation from the ground. Covering him, the Master has placed His outer coat, gently tucking it in here and there.

"Leave me, then," Jesus requests, not looking up.

Iliam, Elob, and the others look at one another with some surprise, but they do not question Jesus. They simply turn and begin to depart.

"You and you," Jesus points to Jessie and to Moira,

"come, be with me." He then glances over quickly to catch the eye of John, whose gaze lovingly embraces His own.

John simply nods and turns to begin climbing the heights to his sacred place. Once at the top, from whence he can see all about, he looks down one last time at his Brother Jesus and his sisters with Him. Then he turns to face north, sits, closes his eyes, and bows his head, resting his hands easily in the lap of his folded legs. The energy comes first as though it were a gentle evening's breeze, and he begins to breathe deeply, rhythmically, gently. The rush of air is audible as he forces it from his body. "So let it be, Lord God. Thy will and Thy peace be with them."

"Seat yourself here, Moira." The Master gestures to a place on the other side of Gideon, whose motionless form apparently rests easily, his countenance serene, yet without any evidence that he is within, only a shallow breathing.

Moira kneels near his head.

"Place your hand there." Jesus points to his forehead.

Moira leans just slightly to extend her arm and places her hand across Gideon's brow. As she glances up to look at Jesus to see if this is correct, a sweetness in His eyes melts her into oneness with Him and with her beloved Gideon.

Jessie has taken a position kneeling less than a meter from Moira's left hand, her hands clasped above her solar plexus. Her eyes are awide, for she is in awe, wonder, that she and her sister should be so honored by this One who bears the Promise.

"With thy left hand, touch the underside of his feet."

Jessie unclasps her hands and shifts her position, moving on her knees to be close to Gideon's feet.

"Hand against the bottoms, touch both with thy left hand," Jesus directs. He nods and softly smiles His approval.

Jesus is on the opposite side at the midsection, the center of Gideon's body. He, too, is kneeling. Sitting very straight, He puts His hands upon His knees and closes His eyes.

In a moment His eyes open. He turns to look up to the place of sacred silence and sees John seated almost precisely as He is. He studies him for but a moment, obviously seeing the Light around him, and then smiles and nods, just slightly, as though to affirm his presence.

He moves back into His silence, and within eternity we can hear, *Come Thou, My Father. Grant unto us the Breath of Life, for this one of faith in Thee. Bring him forth. Let him look upon the paths before him. And I pray thee, Gideon, choose thou life. Thou art loved.*

We move from the eternal silence.

Jesus lifts His head, His eyes open. "Moira, take the right hand of thy sister. Do it now."

Dutifully, Moira glances up to receive Jessie's hand. Their arms are extended just about to the limit, but their fingers entwine, and there is a rush of the love and oneness they share.

Jesus smiles and nods, bowing His head briefly.

In only moments He leans forward without opening His eyes and, stretching His long arms, places one of His hands upon each of His sisters.

It is as though an electric bolt similar to that of a spring storm passes through them all. And though they strive to withhold it, Moira and Jessie gasp at the wonder of it and the stimulation to their bodies, minds, and spirits. They feel the rush of a majestic force flowing through them and the hand in contact with Gideon, so stimulating and energizing that they can barely keep their hands in place, yet they know they must.

"We thank Thee, Lord God. Thy will be done," Jesus murmurs. "Come thou forth, Gideon. Be unto this Light whole that we may give unto thee from the wellspring of our love and faith, which is ever one with you and your brothers." Jesus removes His hands, indicating that Jessie and Moira are to do likewise.

Both maidens rub their hands against their thighs, just above the knees, as though to moderate some aftereffect. Jessie looks from Gideon to Jesus, to Moira, and back to Gideon. Unquestionably, she has been transformed.

Moira is as one spellbound. She cannot remove her eyes from Gideon's face. Her right hand comes up to cover her mouth to stifle a gasp as she sees his eyelids flicker.

Soft sounds come forth, and a hand twitches, an arm moves subtly, a foot wiggles. Then his eyes pop open. He looks about in wonder, stunned at seeing the warm light of Brother Jesus. Glancing to see the two sisters, he works his mouth as though it were a mechanism long forgotten. Tiny words come out. "Well, I see I am in good company."

They laugh with joy at Gideon's humor and the wonder of the miracle that has just been wrought.

The melodious sound of the water cascading down over the rocks and into the sacred pool seems to have a tranquilizing, almost mesmerizing effect upon the Holy Maidens.

"I wonder … Do you think they are still at the School?" Kelleth asks.

"I believe so." Mary nods. "I feel it is so."

"If it were only possible for them to come and visit us, or we them …" Not finishing her sentence, Hannah looks across at Mary.

She turns very slowly to look into Her sister's eyes. The Light passes between them. "I, too," She smiles. "I, too."

"Well, it has been a joy to help prepare the others for their journeys into the outlands," offers Rebekah, with a light note of cheer and humor.

"Ah, and didn't they look splendid?"

"Oh, yes, Abigail, splendid. And how they've grown. Goodness! There is something about their being that seems to shout out, *The Light of God is in me*," adds Little Mary.

"Of course, and we helped light that, too, didn't we?"

All laugh at Zephorah's comment.

"I think we have done quite well," Mary agrees. "Indeed, that which was intended and prophesied has been fulfilled."

None speak further, but simply look down into the pool.

Then Hannah looks up. "Sweet Gideon. … Let us pray for him. Let us ask God that their journey has been good and that our sweet guardian will choose to come back unto us. What sayest thou all?" She glances from one to the other.

"I say yes," Andra offers, as do the others.

"Now is the opportunity to gather those teachings and to bring them to fruition," Elob begins quietly. "Soon we shall go forth. Some of you shall go back unto the lands of the Egyptians. Some of you will go to other ancient places, and the final works that we can give to you will be fulfilled there." He turns to glance at some of the faces. "Others of you will be taken to your place of quiet service, until the time comes that the Promise shall require of you."

John is leaning off to the side against a large rock out-cropping.

Jesus is a pace or so away, seated cross-legged, hands in His lap, body erect, head tilted up slightly, listening carefully, though obviously connected to some spiritual essence that lies beyond this world.

John shifts his position to glance over at James, Phillip, Bartholomew, and Stefan, then across at Moira, Jessie, and finally at all the others. A rush of emotion passes through him and he shifts his body, straightening the folds of his robe as he turns to focus his attention with deliberateness on Elob.

"So for now, let us celebrate with a meditation and a prayer. If you have a question, any at all that remains, bring it forth, that the measure of your cup will be a full one."

He turns to nod at Marta.

She adjusts her body, straightens herself, and places her hands, palms upwards one upon the other on her lap. She tilts her head back, just slightly, closes her eyes and we hear these words: "We are Thy children, Lord God, and now we come unto Thee. We come unto Thee bearing the gift of our joy and love for Thee. Our quest is open. We ask only to give unto Thee and to serve Thee and Thy works. So as Thou perceivest us as righteous, Lord God, speak unto us, that we might know Thy Will and the purpose that is before us, each of us, as we look upon the journey ahead. We claim our oneness with Thee. And, as I speak these sacred names, bring unto each that place which is filled with the righteousness of Thy spirit, that each of us might know Thy peace and Thy joy."

After a pause, Marta speaks, and pauses, and again speaks another name in her native tongue.

Then, the Golden Silence is upon them, one and all.

It would seem as if time has no movement. It would seem as if the elements about them, indeed, the very elements of Earth and nature, have become absolutely passive. It is as if the group were suspended in time and space, wrapped in a comforter of Nothingness. The Allness of it is unmistakable, though. Each of the minds and hearts is open. Occasionally, one notes the Light of the spirit of one of the others of the group. And as each one might so do, they reach out to reaffirm the bond, the path of Light that exists between them … in Earth, and in spirit form. Some of them become illuminated as realizations, guidance, awareness, all of these and greater, are given and received. And so it continues.

Then we hear a soft voice speak. "Unto Thee, Lord God, we give that which we have to give, and in return we receive the presence of Thy spirit so completely that we are ever one. We are filled with the joy, love, peace, and compassion of Your Spirit. The Golden Cup within is, to full measure, complete. We thank You, Lord God. Amen."

The journey is curious as they move continually south along the river's edge. They see many barges and watercrafts pass by in both directions, some propelled by the motion of oars in water, others borne along the current, aided by rudimentary sails. Still others, caravans, camels, and such, also pass. Some of the group acknowledge these travelers, gesturing in specific ways according to the garb and demeanor of those passing by.

James looks over at Phillip, who strides steadily at his side. "It certainly is a great blessing to have the adepts with us on this journey,"

"Yes," Phillip laughs. "We have met no one that one of these adepts could not speak to in their native tongue. Quite amazing." He turns about to look at some of the others. "This has been a long journey. How much further is it, do you suppose?"

"Zelotese said probably two days and one night."

"I shall be glad when we have arrived."

Laughing gently, James turns to look at him again. "Have some apprehension, do you?"

"Well, I do not know that I would call it apprehension, but I certainly feel a sense of anticipation."

James looks ahead and then down at the path they are walking. "It is rather disconcerting, when they describe the initiation as going into death and coming back from it."

They both laugh a bit, albeit with some apprehension slightly evident.

"The purpose is to purify you, not only to wash away the soil of your long journey." Amused, she looks from one to another. They are covered with grime, caked with it, as the perspiration from the long trek through great heat has molded the dust of the earth to conform to their bodies. In some instances when one or another smiles, the soil or grime are so thick that it cracks, as though it were some sort of facial mask intentionally plastered on them. "The priests and priestesses will aid you." She gestures with her hand.

Stefan looks down at the cavities hewn out of the rock and earth itself, and smiles casually. "This is a new one!"

John only looks up quickly and glances at the Master, who is serenely looking about at the great monuments, built, as some say, to honor great kings of the past. But He knows they are much more.

"From whence cometh these, do you think, in truth?" Bartholomew asks.

"From the Ancient Ones. And those of their time," Jesus adds, "but it is the intent of the Ancient Ones. See?" He points to the curves and angles. "When night falls, we shall see them ..." pointing now to the sky, "the doorway into the realms beyond. The guardians, the sentinels, of this time ... they are all connected." Turning to look at his brothers, Jesus continues, "Remember Rebochien's teachings? We shall come face to face with them this evening, I believe."

Their bodies have been bathed, purified, and anointed, and they have been brought clean garments. They are gathered around the evening's fire, having meditated and prayed for long hours. They ingest only the bare essentials to meet and sustain their bodies' needs. No solids, only a bit of fluids.

"When the alignment is correct," Zelotese begins softly, "we shall start. Speak now, if you have a concern, or question. Or if you would step away from this, then say it. There is naught but honor here for all of you. But this choice is a crossroads. Therefore, we must hear your affirmation spoken aloud."

First one affirms, "I choose to go forth." Then the next does the same, and the next, until all have confirmed that they choose the journey ahead.

"Rest now and claim your oneness ... unify your spirit, mind, heart, and body. It is well for you to do this. But, most importantly, find your place of peace. It is from the peace of your oneness that the journey ahead shall begin."

It is sometimes written that in the journey called life there are events of sufficient magnitude to transform what shall come thereafter. Very often these crossroads are met and not carefully seen or not evaluated from a place of peace. Rather, they are influenced by the decision that follows, by the thoughts or emotions that are preponderant in that time, that moment.

We encourage you, then, dear friends, to ever be at such a place that your spirit is not set aside, but ever open and aware, not to the diminishment of mind, heart, and emotion, but to their enhancement.

What lies ahead for these beautiful souls and Our Lord is the portal through which, once they have entered it, certain aspects of their being will be transformed. Portions of what they have known will fall away in terms of import and relevance, and the awakening of the Promise as it applies to each shall manifest.

Chapter Five

Anointed of God

*I*nitially, the darkness is so complete that it seems as if there is no light at all. But soon, as the physical eyes become better adjusted, soft, almost imperceptible light becomes visible. Slowly the silhouettes of the others can be distinguished in the surrounding sea of darkness.

Time has passed, brief by some standards, but lengthy in terms of encountering that which is foreign, unknown, to the candidates, both the Essenes and the adepts of the School, all of whom are about to claim and move into the Light.

One of the Essenes whispers to the one next to him, "This is odd, unlike anything we have experienced previously. What thoughts have you?"

"I think, Thomas, that we should remain silent," Moira responds, somewhat playfully but with a serious tone.

"I suppose you are right. But the darkness and silence … Do they not feel rather heavy to you?"

There is a substantial pause. Then with a bit of amusement in her voice, she answers. "Different, more intense than I have perhaps noticed in the past. But not heavy."

"I see." Thomas lets out a sigh and moves back into the silence.

This chamber is quite sizable and is but one of many which lie beneath ground level near the Three Temples, as they are referred to by those who dwell here. The preparations for purification and the movement of the candidates from both sectors have brought them to this point.

Footsteps sound. One cannot distinguish precisely the number of candidates approaching, but even in this incredible stillness and near darkness, they stand out, though they are filing in barefoot.

"We greet you, brothers and sisters," a beautiful voice begins. "It is a part of the sacred rituals that you be brought into your awakening and the preparation for what lies ahead in this manner."

We hear a single clap of hands, and light begins to grow off in the distance. Soon several who are clothed in unique garments bear small oil lamps into the chamber.

With the light, everyone looks about this way and that, recognizing a dear brother or sister, adepts nodding to the Essene candidates, and so forth.

The chamber is largely square and with the barest essentials … seating apparati, but that is about all. Light from the oil lamps glistens on the shaven head of the figure in the center. A long clump of hair hangs down his back, interwoven with some fibers and other indistinguishable items.

"I am called Sephara by my brothers and sisters. I shall speak to you largely as one who strives to serve. While some of our ways may seem foreign to you, it is our prayer that you will find them purposeful, of service to you and even of some familiarity to you through the skills you have acquired and experiences you have passed through. You will see that our ways carry the same truths as all that you have learned to the present."

Sephara looks about the group, silently meeting each pair of eyes that is fixed upon him with anticipation in a swift, but complete exchange. Gesturing to many of his assistants, Sephara introduces them and the nature of that which they have chosen as the gift of service each can provide to the candidates. They, in turn, rise and turn slowly, smiling gently in the same manner, to silently greet each one here. This continues for a goodly while.

After a time, Sephara rises and calls the candidates to follow him. He moves along curious passageways, bypassing small chambers. Here and there an entry is covered. Some are open, and as the candidates file by, they can see figures in the dim light within. Other chambers contain small lamps with figures seated around them in silence, or in chant.

The passageway begins to move upwards. While darkness has fallen and no moon lights the sky, the transition from the darkness of the passageway, even with a few oil lamps present, is striking, for the brilliance of the evening stars is profound.

The candidates move about as Sephara continues to stride forward, followed by many of his assistants. Then, with a nod from him, they guide each of the candidates to take a position, forming a semi-circle. Without speaking, he turns to gesture upwards, indicating the familiar alignments.

Jessie leans to Moira and whispers softly, "How clear and brilliant our heavenly brothers' and sisters' light is here."

Moira looks up smiling, and simply nods.

Sephara then points to the first great monument, which is very near to where they are positioned. "You will find that this temple is aligned to match the flow of energies and alignments of Earth's power so perfectly that when you are within this temple and your Initiation has begun, you will move beyond time itself. You will feel the essences of all those forces that are of the womb of creation flowing into the Earth. And you will be able to look beyond these into what some call the timeless void of the past, and then into the light of the future.

"But in that which shall follow, you will find, as you have had a small sampling this evening in our sacred chamber below," he points down, "that this is only the first step. We are honored to have you and pray that what we offer, and what lies ahead, will bring you an awakening ..." he turns, looking where Jesus and several of the others with Him are seated, "and that your gifts that you, all of you, will undoubtedly bring forth in this Initiation shall merge with ours to become a force of Light offered to the Earth, now and forever ... that those who would seek might know that here, through the reflection of the light of their own brothers and sisters and the gifts left for us all by the Ancients, is the pathway to truth. Some of you will discover and, as you choose to claim it, will be given the gift of Righteousness. I say, on behalf of all of our peoples," he extends his arms, "ever, are we with you in that work."

"We are aware that not much has been given to you regarding what shall transpire here and what the process shall be like. In answer to some of your questions, each of you will be given an opportunity to find the opening, often referred to as the Portal of Light, or Golden Door within you. When you find it in your own chamber of Spirit, which shall take place in one of the physical chambers you have seen below," again he points downwards, "then one or more of us will come to you and guide you through it. You will know when you are ready. And then shall come your passage into this Temple," he gestures to the Great Pyramid before them, "and you shall be brought to the Veil of Separateness in the upper chamber. What will follow, only you shall know.

"Upon its completion, you will tell us what shall transpire next in the new life that will appear before you thereafter. And we will give to you all that we are and have to fulfill that. Thereafter, some of you will go independently into that new life. Others will go perhaps two or more together to the work that follows. All of you will become teachers in ways that you cannot at this time fully comprehend." Turning to smile at Jesus and several of the others, Sephara comments in closing, "At least, that's true for most of you."

Jesus only smiles softly and nods, entirely at ease, legs

folded beneath Him, hands resting in the outer garments of His lap.

The sun is very warm as they stroll around the perimeter almost casually, as though they were mere travelers or passersby. This is by the intent of the priests and priestesses of the Temple of Initiation. The candidates pause here and there to reflect upon all that they are being taught and to exchange examples and perspectives they have encountered through inner reflection in their sacred quest in the chambers beneath the earth. Some are more serious and studious; others are light, excited, vibrant.

To the southwest corner of the great monument, we find a number of large stones, seemingly oddly placed, for the rest of the terrain is largely barren, except for the structures on the other side.

"When do you think you will enter it?" Jessie asks the Master, gesturing to the Great Temple.

Hands resting on His knees as He is seated upon a huge stone, Jesus smiles and looks down, stretching out His foot to toy with a pebble. After a pause, He looks up serenely. "I believe soon, my good sister. Very soon."

The look in His eyes is such that Jessie does not follow up with other comments or questions. She studies His face, joyfully noting the emergence of a serenity surpassing the love and compassionate understanding that she and all of her brothers and sisters recognize and cherish as characteristic of the Master.

He leans back, stretching and looking about. Resting one hand on His left knee, He rubs the side of His face as though reflecting, His eyes bright and sparkling. "And so, James, how do you assess all this?"

James, broken out of a bit of inner reflection, glances about and chuckles softly. "Forgive me, I ... "

The Master simply nods and raises a hand indicating, *No*

need to explain. I know where you were.

"I think it is remarkable that there could be such planning and design. I know not if you have visited it, Brother, but the records and the writings of the designs of the universe and such, they are …" James straightens himself and breathes in deeply, "stunning. To think of such foresight and planning, such calculations in a time that no one even knows about save the mystics, the teachers, and the seers! But I mean in the outer world, no one knows about this."

"Well, I know that that is not completely so. But I share your delight in the purity of spirit of those who claimed truth and recorded it here." Jesus gestures to the monument of stone. "Here, for all to see who can see, and in the sacred chambers that you so revere. But I know, dear brother, as I might remind you to know as well, many have experienced these truths and have translated them according to the beauty of their own uniqueness and their people's truths. To demonstrate this to you, I remind you of our journey not that long ago to the Great Library, wherein I saw the same fire of joy and excitement of discovery flowing from your eyes and evident in your words."

James smiles expansively, but simply nods, bringing a hand up to rub his chin. Resting that elbow upon his folded arm, he closes his eyes and rocks as he journeys within to explore the memories of those truths.

The Light around the man called Jesus is brilliant. As He emerges from the portal of the Great Temple, Sephara and all those with him wait, seated cross-legged in a pattern of their own design, formed by their physical bodies. Only these adepts are present to greet Him.

The Master pauses before them and looks around.

Sephara rises and comes to within a dozen paces before Him, bows, hands thrust into his garments that they cannot be seen, and slowly bends to kneel, head bowed. "Thou Anointed One of God, grant us Thy blessing. Tell us … How may we serve Thee?"

Jesus' gaze is so warming it invokes sighs and blissful smiles from those of Sephara's peoples who are gathered. Some close their eyes and nod in gratitude to the Master. Others raise their hands in gestures unique to them, knowing that the Anointed One will see their precise intent.

"I would be aided to journey from here now," the Master begins gently. "I must sup of my spirit. It is a time that I must become complete in that which is the gift of thy hospitality and teaching. Wouldst thou help me in this intent?"

As though this request has been anticipated, several of Sephara's peoples with bundles over their arms and shoulders move swiftly and, bowing to the Master, receive His bow in return. Wordlessly they move rapidly off to the north, away from the Temples and into the wilderness.

The Master follows. All watch as their brothers and sisters and the Anointed One diminish upon the horizon.

In the stillness of the night their footsteps are all that can be heard, and seem to create an accompanying vision.

As we look upon them, we hear Moira speaking to the adepts who are with this group. "It has been a blessing, no doubt eternal, unto us all … a blessing that will be like one of those," she points to the stars above, "but upon our very spirits." She turns to look at her brothers and sisters who are a part of the entourage that is moving back through the wilderness, towards the great School.

"We share that same joyful thought," acknowledges one of the adepts.

They all fall silent as they continue their journey.

Having arrived at the great School, they are gathered around the flames of a beautiful fire. Nourished and cleansed in their tradition of purification and the rituals of their faith, each one offers prayers for those who have not been seen for great periods of time.

"The preparations have been made," explains Iliam softly, "to carry and provide for you on your journeys tomorrow. Those of you who will return to your peoples and begin your teachings, remember that we are oft in prayer with you. Carry with you our love and our blessings." He glances around the group as he speaks.

There is a long silence followed by comments, exchanges of gratitude and blessing, and loving reminiscences of the events and discoveries that they shared over the past year.

"Who is it that we are going to teach?" asks Thomas quietly.

"Your brethren, those who have been a part of the works in other locations of your peoples who have been brought back into the outer world, and now await your presence."

"You mean we are to teach our own peoples?"

"Who better?" answers Elob.

Thomas looks down and fingers the earth before him.

"I find it incredibly joyful to contemplate sharing these beautiful gifts we have been given," Moira announces, blissfully spreading her arms wide.

"Oh, I too." Jessie agrees, but is much more subdued.

"How will they come to know that what we offer them is of truth?"

Zelotese rises and walks over to the fire, adding a bit of fuel. Brushing his outer garment, he turns to answer Bartholomew. "By the Light of truth that is within you, of course. By the awakened spirit that has become one with the spirit of this life, so that upon the Golden Pathway between your spirit and you can flow, as you are willing, all that is needed. Indeed, these things you know. As your brother Jesus might well say to you at this point, *Bartholomew, dost thou test this? Or seek to make it a certainty?*" Zelotese, hands on his hips, is bending a bit and smiling broadly.

Bartholomew laughs heartily at the realization that Zelotese's words are utterly true. He does know these things, and the light within has, indeed, been awakened.

In the morning's light, a lone figure can barely be seen atop Reflection Rock.

Leaning back as he gazes up, Iliam sighs deeply, looks down, and slowly walks off to the side. Suddenly, a tiny pebble strikes the boulder to his right. Startled, he stops, spots it, and a warm smile sweeps over his face. Returning his gaze to the top of the rock, he sees that figure now has an arm raised. It moves slowly down so the hand can cover the heart, and then extends out to gesture to Iliam, evidencing the love felt. It is a love he clearly shares and returns a thousand-fold to John.

Later, after they have reenacted the morning ritual and visited the spirits of their brothers and sisters whose journeys have begun elsewhere, they begin gathering their things in preparation for their own journey ahead.

The adepts move about, touching, embracing, presenting this one or that with tiny gifts intended to be blessings to the ones with whom they have shared special times, times which the Light of Life has recorded in the fabric of the Universe itself, that the joy shared shall remain eternally written upon the very Robe of God.

"Unto where shall you journey, John?"

Seated upon a small rock, a stout staff over one shoulder, a small bundle swinging from its end, John studies the earth before glancing up at Iliam. "I believe I shall go and visit some of my old friends."

Iliam's brows arch in question. "Might I know them?"

"I am certain you would know those whom I know."

"From whence come these friends, then, dear John?"

"From the life force eternal. While I have not seen them

in present form, I know their spirits, and I know that their spirits await our reuniting in this new time, these new places." He sweeps his arm, broadly gesturing. "I shall seek, as ever, the clearer guidance of our Lord God. I have not seen beyond certain veils in my meditation and prayer, but these friends call to me and so I shall seek them."

Iliam nods, smiling, but with a hint of sadness.

John notes this instantly and responds, "I, too, Iliam, my brother, feel what you feel. But, as you, I know distance can never separate us. The joy that I hold here for you," he taps on his chest, "will always sustain me. And if that is not enough, I shall come to visit you in this," now slapping his chest with the palm of his hand, "in the flesh, often."

They rise and embrace, then stand with their hands upon one another's shoulder for a brief moment or two. Their eyes seem intertwined, as if embracing as their bodies did only a moment ago.

Not another word is spoken. John quickly grasps his staff and its small bundle, turns, and strides through the all-too-familiar passageway.

Iliam recalls that it was here he had searched for the missing John that one morning not so long ago, and found not just him, but the line of light that exists eternally between the two, forever.

"Many of them have been returned to the outer world." Judy glances around the group present.

"Have you visited them?" Bartholomew asks.

"Yes, on a goodly number of occasions," Mary interjects. "We have, many of us, established ourselves in the outer world, as you are intended to do now as you go forth."

"How do we interact with them? How do we build a life in the outer world?" Thomas asks quietly, a hint of emotion evident in his voice.

"Why do you have to build a life, Thomas?" Kelleth responds, rather sharply.

"Well, the life that I know, at this point, does not match their lives."

"Why not? Have you not gone beyond that yet?" Kelleth laughs heartily.

Thomas shares her laughter but then counters, "I guess it is that these two, could I call them, worlds of consciousness are so different. And I suppose the intent of my question is to ask if you have any suggestions."

Many laugh at this.

"I have one," Hannah responds gently, her head playfully tossed to the side.

"What is that?"

"Do not talk too much. Listen … a lot!"

There is a brief silence, and then everyone laughs cheerfully, for all know that Thomas is quick to express a question, a counterpoint, and all such. But no one fails one whit to hold him in absolute fondness and love, for the sincerity of his spirit's quest for truth is beyond question.

"Where did John go?" Bartholomew asks.

"Yes," adds James, "I miss him a great deal."

"Well, I am certain that soon enough you will see or hear of him." And with considerable laughter Andra continues, "In fact, you might have a moment or two wherein you wish you had not." She throws her head back, and her mighty laugh fills the area where they are gathered.

"Really?" James responds, caught up in her laughter. "Could I ask what you mean by that?"

Andra glances at her sisters and the teachers.

Anna, smiling gently, is seated comfortably, watching with love and pride in the accomplishments of these whom she calls her children as well as her brothers and sisters. "Well, we have seen your brother John to be in a work that will challenge the core of many existing standards, and may call some attention to him. And … well, you will see. It is likely that his will be as a voice calling out in the wilderness, where no voices are ever expected to be heard."

The sisters look at one another, smile, but say no more. Some get a distant, wistful look in their eyes. Others look this way and that and reach out to take one another's hands. For Judy and Anna have seen much that lies ahead, and the other seers and prophets have added to this. More, when John, the Master and many of the others would return and recount their dreams and visions after meditations and times of fasting, much of the future was made clear.

They embrace mightily, for it has been nearly their entire lifetime since they have seen one another.

"James, I cannot tell you how often the others of our holy family have spoken of you, and of our brothers and sisters. But to have you here and to touch you physically, I praise God for this great blessing."

Arm in arm, hands locked at each other's elbows, as is the custom, James smiles from his very spirit. "I have often thought of you, my brother, and, oh, what I have to share with you!"

"Well, come then, James!" John responds. "Come, let us sit and take tea. Let us begin. We have been given much, shared much in our teachings, but we all know He was actually *with* you."

"You will see Him. This I promise you."

Judas listens tearfully as Thomas, his spiritual brother, shares recent background events with him. Looking down and adjusting the colorful garments that he wears, Judas shifts the implements before them. A tear traces down the side of his face following a path, it would seem, intended just for it to travel. "How did he heal Justus? Tell me of it. Leave nothing out, tell me it all."

Thomas begins, love clearly pouring through his words,

his eyes closed and hands gesturing. Finally, he concludes the story. "And He placed a hand here, like this. You see? And another here. And He was but a lad! And the withered leg became whole."

Judas strikes his chest again and again with his clenched fist. "I praise Thee, God. It is I, Judas. I send unto You all glory, for Thy Promise has come. Let me be that, as Thou wouldst have me be ... to serve Thee and Him."

The table is simple, but sturdy. On it sit several baskets of bread and traditional broths for dipping. A knife and board rest here, too, upon which sit the cheese and several flasks.

"Where did He go?" Mark asks Bartholomew.

"Unto the east, we are told. He came not back unto the School, but began His journey. The last who saw Him was Sephara and his peoples who, we are told, guided Him to the great city of knowledge by the Sea, the Library. Several of the adepts ... who are masters, mind you ... joined them, some who had traveled from the east, to guide Him. And now, they have begun the journey, the work."

"None of you, our brothers and sisters, saw Him afterwards?" asks Luke.

"None. It has been said that one of the group might have watched from a distance. But none were present."

"Who is that one?"

"Brother John, for he was absent and none knew where he was. He spoke it not, but one of Sephara's people indicated that it might be so."

"Did you question John about this?" Mark asks.

"No. He departed as well. But when we joined him again at the great School ... Well, it was not appropriate."

They look at one another and nod.

"What have you been taught?"

"We are told much the same as you all, Bartholomew," Mark responds. "But we are told that the completion of this will come from you and perhaps others of our brothers and sisters. Other than that, we are not certain where it shall come from, except from Jesus … upon His return, I suspect."

"It is likely so." Bartholomew turns to look at Jessie, who has been silent the whole while. "It has been said that you were a part of the healing work with Our Lord. Is that true?"

A light comes upon her and shines through her eyes. "It is true." She looks down at her hands as she turns them palms up to study them. "Through these hands, and Moira's, He did the work. I and my sister were one with Him."

"Can you give of this to us, that we might do likewise, should a need arise?" Luke asks gently.

"I shall give all that I have to give. But I know not if it shall come to pass that such works can be done in the same manner, without His being present."

So it continues as all of those who are to walk with Him are called forth and given that needed for their awakening and the completion of their journey to this point.

As many months unfold, each of these who have returned share what they have learned with their brothers and sisters, who in turn give what they have that those who have returned can become knowledgeable and one with the outer world. And when they are called to serve, they shall each be ready.

"How wonderful to have you here with us again, John!"

"And for me with thee." His now oddly attired body is stretched out casually in a reclining position, arm propped up on a sizeable rock beneath his head.

"We have heard many fascinating stories from diverse places." That familiar sparkle is in Andra's eyes, the one that John remembers and so very dearly.

"What stories might these be?" he asks, smiling.

"Oh, that many travelers have found you here and there,

as though you appeared suddenly from nowhere, in the midst of the wilderness."

"Ah." He is still smiling, but offers no explanation.

"And others have heard you by the river, speaking of things to come."

"Yes, by the river," he confirms softly.

"Well?" Smiling coyly, Andra leans toward John. "Have any of these the leaven of truth in them?"

John straightens up, his legs crossed, the wooly-looking outer garment making him look almost animal-like, to the great delight of all of the Holy Maidens, who can see the spirit of this one coming forth, not only from within but literally upon his body.

"I would suppose that what they have spoken is their perception of truth. The literal truth, perhaps, might have some variances here and there." He laughs quietly. "But for the most part, that which you have recounted here does bear the leaven of truth in it."

"Why do you not come here and stay with us, John?" asks one of the other Maidens, wistfully voicing the thoughts of many.

He looks at her with sincerity. "To what end?"

"We miss you."

"Well, we all miss someone," John begins gently, "until we look within and find our memory of them, just as He taught. Remember? All of you were there when He thumped me on the chest and said, *If you hold me here, I will always be with you.* Well, that is His truth and I accept it and I yet hold it here." John thumps himself on the chest. "Perhaps it would be good for you to do the same when remembering me and all of our brothers and sisters."

Little Sophie shakes her head and smiles. "Well, it is not the same as looking upon you, John," and she, too, laughs.

"When do you think that He will return?"

Mary does not turn, but continues to stir the evening's meal in the cooking pot. "They say it will yet be some time, my dear husband. But they also say that He will return and dwell with us for a while before He begins the work." Brushing Her hands off on a bit of cloth, She turns to walk over and seat Herself beside Joseph.

She reaches down to pick up his hand and kisses the back of it. "I know He will be with you, at least for a time, for you are deserving of a great gift of God. And He, this I hear in my heart, is the only one who can give it to you."

His eyes fixed upon the cookflame beneath the pot Mary has just been stirring, Joseph smiles.

"There is a lot of controversy," Nicodemus confides, "and I mean a lot. Word has gotten out, in no small part due to the Forerunner." Nicodemus smiles, then strikes his chest several times and continues, "God's Spirit be upon him and surround him with God's Peace." Then he shakes his head. "I am not so certain he is wisely advised to speak as he does."

Simon looks up at him. "I know. I know just whereof you speak." He turns to look at Judy whose form appears slighter now. "What say you, sweet teacher?"

Studying the space between them as though it were telling her something, she looks up. "It is the prophecy, and he is hearing it and following it by the light of his own spirit. As a people, we can become divided on this issue. Or we can unite and trust in the light that shines in him as in all of the chosen ones, our brothers and sisters, that same Light which shines on and through Our Lord."

"There is something to be said about recognizing the nature of the outer world, however." Nicodemus chuckles, then adds more soberly, "I expect that before long, they may seek to silence that voice in the wilderness."

"We cannot allow him to continue as he is," Moesha insists quietly. "The peoples of our tribes have become fearful again. For so long, we have not been sought nor persecuted. But, surely, if he continues, they will turn against us again. Ask him to be silent. Soon enough the Light will return from the East, and that will be sufficient."

"You would have us say unto John, *Be silent*?" Anna looks around and begins to laugh incredulously. "First of all, if anyone could find him when they wanted to, that would be quite a gift of God, a miracle indeed. For they are saying he appears and disappears whenever he wishes. While we do not know that to be of truth, we do know that he is unique in many ways. You would have us countermand the guidance that he hears within?"

Laughing amiably, Andra speaks out. "Truly Moesha, you know John not, else you would not say this to us."

Swiftly rising to his feet, as do those who have accompanied him, Moesha admonishes them in a harsh, tone. "Then I tell you this … We shall withdraw our alliance!"

The sisters gasp and look at one another.

"Not only our peoples', but several of the other tribes as well! He is not the Promise! By what right speaketh he such things? By what right can he forgive them of sin?"

The silence that follows has a sweetness that seems utterly foreign. The teachers, the sisters, the seers, all gathered, including the remaining elders, seem to have known that this was to come, that a division between light and darkness, truth and illusion, exists in all peoples as a potential. And, indeed, many of those here had seen and foretold that it might, truly, separate this house so dedicated unto God and so focused upon doing His Works.

"We wish you all blessings, of course, and the Peace of God to be upon and with you. We tell you these things not idly, but after searching our hearts, our spirits, we shall stand back from the choice and path of this one and from you, our dear brothers and sisters, because you have aligned yourselves with him. We do this not in judgment, but because we believe it righteous and because we believe unto the Promise that shall come, and that alone! Thus do we deem it wise to preserve our peoples in their entirety for that time when He shall come forth. We shall move our villages unto new locales, and we shall seek not to join in your holy works, ceremonies, and celebrations, lest such comings together be found and we *all* perish at the hands of those who would take the Promise from the Earth."

When you journey into your hearts and find that place of wondrous silence, and you ask, and listen, to hear the truth that is ever present in that great temple, bringing it forth into the outer self is a journey of challenge. For the inner truth will bypass those facets of the self that will question and probe, doubt and fear. Your other facets – like a people combined into one individual – shall also speak, saying such as: Have faith. Hold to the Light. Believe unto the Promise. Believe unto thy brother and sister.

It is that journey from the sacred temple within you, the traveling of truth from the inner to the outer, that lies before you in these very days in Earth.

So we say unto you, as our brothers and sisters, and in that Light of God's love: Have faith. The truth from within self is of God.

Chapter Six

The Time Draws Nigh

In the darkness of this eventide, as we look down below us we can see clusters of dwellings. In the distance lies the temple. As we move downwards, we see a lane, a pathway between the structures and two solitary figures moving silently.

The night is dark. Only a bit of light can be seen sporadically beneath some doorways. Still the figures move silently, swiftly, with a sense of surety about them. Rounding a corner and proceeding down another lane, they come before a goodly doorway. One figure reaches out to knock. Slowly, the door opens and there stands Nicodemus. His face breaks into a great smile as he looks upon the Master and John and calls them within. As we move with them into the first chamber, let us describe it for you so you can be here with them.

Nicodemus has moved to the center of the room after embracing each of them in the custom of the Essenes. To our left is the hearth, embers and small flames still dancing their light upon the mantel. More soft lighting comes from several oil lamps in this moderate to large L-shaped room. To our right, we see others seated and an array of small objects placed here and there. The great walls are smooth, plastered, but every so often a bit of their underlying wooden framework can be seen.

The Master and John stand in the entryway. As they remove their head coverings and look about smiling with obvious joy to be here, they see Mary and two of the Maidens tending the cookfire and that which is being prepared upon it.

When Mary turns and sees Him, She smiles and stands with arms open to receive Him. He returns Her smile with the unequivocal warmth of a love that is timeless and strides to Her. As they embrace, He looks down upon Her face, up-turned to meet His. Tears of joy can be seen glistening in the lamplight. Slowly, smiling all the while, the Master kisses them and both sides of Her face, then holds Her at arm's-length, Her arms resting upon His. "My heart rejoices to look upon you again."

Nodding wordlessly, She reaches up to kiss Him on each cheek, and they embrace for several more long moments. As they separate, His hand rests upon the side of Her head. She leans into His touch and their eyes close for a moment, and then they look upon each other once again and simply smile.

Then Mary pulls Hannah and Sophie to Her, who have been standing at Her side, and He receives them similarly, touching their cheeks with a gentle movement of His hand, His thumb wiping away a tear, kissing them upon their foreheads. Each of the Maidens takes one of His hands, and He turns to look at Mary, whose hands are upon Her heart.

"Ahem." John stands immediately before Mary, his arms outstretched expansively.

She rushes to him and they lock one another in a great embrace. Speaking softly, they touch each other's face, and smile. Hannah and Sophie have released the Master hands and He has stepped back so they can greet John, as well.

Others have now entered from the center courtyard and from the dwelling and sleeping chambers that lie beyond it. The Master and John stride forward to greet each of them.

All the while, hands folded before him, Nicodemus has stood smiling in great joy, pride, and wonder at the blessings that have been brought to his home.

Jesus is speaking softly with Theresa, and John is laughing with Nathanael, who has come bearing an armload of scrolls, excitedly recounting how they have been brought here from the distant lands.

To the side is Miriam, shy, awaiting her opportunity to greet the guests who have come from such a distance to join in this great celebration. John turns to walk over to her, and they stand holding hands for a moment and then embrace, as he relates news from her homeland, and the Master comes with a sweep of first one arm and then another, embracing them both, laughing all the while.

Now Eloise and Hannah step forward bearing great bowls of warm broth.

John strides swiftly over, bends to catch the aroma, and then stands. "Fit for a king, or perhaps two of them," and laughs heartily.

The Master comes, too, to savor the aroma of the herbs and such, which He knows have been harvested with much joy and prepared by these Maidens, whose faith and love and compassion are unequaled.

John steps back and motions for the Master to take the bowl that Hannah has extended. With a simple smile, He places a hand over each of hers and looks into her eyes. "My blessings to these hands which have so lovingly prepared and now give this gift."

Touched by His blessing, Hannah looks down, and when He takes the bowl from her hands, she places them over her heart, as did Our Lady, bows her head, and steps back.

Theresa comes forward with an offering for John, who cants his head to one side. "The beauty of your being is wondrous. And look. Look at what you bring Jesus and me … another gift worthy of the greatest of all to consume. You honor me, and I thank you."

Shyly, struggling to suppress a giggle, Theresa places her hands over her heart, bows her head, and steps back.

"And the rest of you," the Master calls to the others,

"will you not join us? Or have you already partaken?"

Some come forward, for they, too, have only recently arrived, while others simply gesture for the Master and John to seat themselves out in the courtyard. More lamps are scattered on the colonnades, their flames dancing, flickering, casting shadows as though of unseen souls celebrating this event, of which John surmises, "Maybe the shadows are the occasional passing of the wings of angels who wish to be present, as well."

The Master has seated himself between Thaddeus and Nicodemus. At the other end of the long table John speaks with several of the Maidens and with Aromanis who has come from the Far East, and asks him about his journey and the events in his homeland.

Someone brings a great scroll with ornate wooden handles. Aromanis unrolls it and in a warm yet strong voice points out the movement of the spheres to John, the castings and calculations that Aromanis himself and others with him have made.

As he continues, John looks up to catch the gaze of the Master, who is listening to the conversation. Their eyes lock for a moment or two and their faces grow solemn. Standing a few paces behind Him, Mary observes this and raises Her hands to Her heart again. Her eyes close and Her head bows in what is obviously a silent prayer. As we glance about, we see the other Maidens scattered all about the large courtyard simultaneously doing the same, as though some unspoken command had been given. After a moment, the Maidens and Mary end their silent prayer, and move about.

Time passes, and various exchanges take place here and there. Then, there is a soft knock.

Nicodemus rises swiftly and peering out the doorway welcomes one more to the gathering. His laughter quickly identifies the new arrival as Jacob.

He strides directly into the courtyard. The Master and

John immediately rise and welcome him with the typical Essene gesture. All three then collide in a massive embrace so generous in manner that in this muted light one might have difficulty telling which arm belongs to whom, and which bit of laughter comes from which individual.

When they finally end their embrace, Jacob extends his arms and then claps his hands. No more is needed. John, the Master, and Jacob, with hands upon each other's shoulders, start their little dance. Softly, Jacob begins a song known by all here, for they have heard it from childhood on. The Master and John join in, then He looks about and gestures, and others rise, first shyly, then exuberantly. John, Jacob, and Jesus release one another, allowing others to move between them and place their arms about these to join the dance.

The Maidens then gather 'round this group and, reaching out, grasp one another's hands, forming their own circle, and dance. They add their voices, which rise in joyful song.

Shortly thereafter, without stopping his movement, Jacob raises his hands and offers a prayer. He ends the prayer with a great laugh of joy, and gestures for the Maidens. The group opens and the two groups become one.

John leans his head to rest on Hannah's as he feels the warmth of her hand resting on the back of his neck. He turns to look upon her. "I have missed you."

She returns his gaze. "I know you know that we have never truly been apart, but it is so good to see you this way."

With arms yet upon the shoulders of those to either side, Jesus asks, "Who has a prayer? Who has a need?"

Sophie steps into the circle and with a sure, clear voice states, "I have a prayer, Lord."

"Speak it, then," He answers, smiling broadly.

She raises her hands, closes her eyes and moves around in a silent circle. Her hands are now close together, flowing this way and that, still upraised. She moves about the group as they continue with their dance and song. Softly, she offers her need on behalf of one she knows is in a state of dis-ease. Then, glancing up as she completes her work, she sees that the Master is gazing at her lovingly.

He smiles and nods to indicate that the work is done.

The dance continues, and He speaks again. "Who shall be next? What needs are there? Let us fill them."

Nicodemus now steps forward. Dancing a bit, bobbing up and down a little awkwardly because of his stature in the community, he reorients himself to become one with this profoundly loving and compassionate group. Emulating Sophie, he raises his hands, closes his eyes, and bobs his head to and fro. "Lord God, grant me Thy wisdom as I seek to serve our people and Thy work." Moving in a small circle, he continues naming those whom he represents before the council.

The Master moves His head to and fro, and as Nicodemus states a name, the Master repeats it.

John echoes it immediately, as do all the others, as though to speak the name is to grant the request.

So it continues, with others coming forth here and there.

When they finally conclude, they all take positions seated in a circle.

The Master moves to the center. He raises His outstretched arms and turns, His eyes shining in the lamplight. His smile embraces each one as He speaks their name, forming an eternal bond with each in turn.

When all have been greeted equally so by the Master, His head bows, and we hear this prayer: "Father, it is I. Thank You for this living temple that I know shall long endure, bearing Thy Word forth to all who would hear it. In that time which lies beyond the twilight of this life, may they, as they journey into same, remember who they are. Bless them, Father, as they have blessed me with the living temple of their love and compassion. Selah! Holy is each."

A long pause follows.

The Master lifts His head, hands now together upon His breast. He turns slowly once again, not speaking this time, but allowing His spirit to again touch each one, as though to say, *We are ever one. Bear this forth, the truth of who and what you are. Carry it ever as that joy which sustains you through all.*

It is Rebekah who stands, raises her hands, claps them, and with her head moving to and fro, swirls about slowly in a circle, chanting her truth. One by one, the other Maidens rise and do the same. As we look about the gathering, we see beautiful rays of light come forth from each of the Maidens as they offer their truth, their gift, to the Christ.

Jesus turns to gesture to John, who rises and spryly strides to stand beside Him. Then He turns in the other direction and calls Nathanael, Jacob, Nicodemus, and all the others.

The Maidens are scattered about, twirling, singing, laughing. Those whom they encircle begin to laugh, as well.

Mary moves to stand before the Master, who once again looks down upon Her upturned face, and they gently gaze at one another for a few moments. Then Her hands come up, and the Maidens stop immediately to join Her.

Our Lady speaks, rocking slightly as She does. "These are my Sisters. We are one. While my body has borne the flesh in which Your spirit shines, yet has each of these equally given to You. And now, as they have proclaimed their gifts to You once again, we come together in this time of oneness in a sisterhood of promise to give to You who are the Son of God and of my body, as well.

"We pledge to You the promise of our gift's endurance. We shall carry it into the twilight of which You have spoken in prayer. And as we, too, enter therein, we shall nurture these gifts, care for them, as though they are borne within our very womb … not the womb of flesh, but the womb of spirit. And we, as the keepers of our gifts, await Your dawning. In that time as shall come to pass, we shall go before You, bearing our gifts. And those who are unseen but known to be with us, whom we call the Ancients and those of you whom we are now honoring shall find unto your need in those times ahead, that the Promise can be fulfilled. We shall come into the Earth again to await You. Now, we hold You ever in our hearts as well as in the heart of hearts, which is eternal."

Stepping back and extending their arms, once again the Maidens encircle the group, barely touching at the fingertips, for it is large. They move slowly and deliberately, turning their heads with each step to look at each other, as though to form an eternal memory of this moment and their oneness. The Master raises His hands in a silent blessing. John and all the others do the same.

A veritable glow of light begins to emanate from the circle of Maidens. With eyes closed, those encircled by them feel it, know it. Slowly their hands, led by the Master's own, rise upwards, as though they are receiving special blessings from the growing shaft of light created by the Maidens, blessings which are bestowed upon each one.

As they complete the ritual, the Maidens are still holding hands, but are turned to face the group and the Master. The Master once more reaches a hand up, placing it upon Mary's cheek. She leans into it and their eyes close for a moment.

Softly, the Master speaks to Her. "Thank you for your gift. You have empowered me to endure that which we all know lies ahead."

Mary bends Her head towards Him, and He kisses Her forehead. …

He then moves to Eloise, thanking her for her gift.

Then to Hannah, whose eyes shine with expectancy. He places a hand upon her cheek and thanks her for her gift.

And Theresa, whose smile is so contagious, and Rebekah, and Miriam, and the little one He calls Sophie … All about the group, so it goes.

Finally, all seat themselves.

Jacob stands and extends his arms, so characteristic of him. But this time there is no dance, no song. He turns slowly, his eyes powerful, filled with light. "We must begin. The time draws nigh. Each of us must bear that part within which is holy. As we give this from the fullness of our own cup, so is it ever replenished. Let us keep the sacred chalice of oneness with God pure and full. Let us be hopeful, let us be loving and compassionate. Let us ever seek truth and honor, and hold them bound together with the power of our faith, the faith that comes from oneness, not separateness. This power is borne in the completeness of that which we have claimed, that which we hold, as the Master has given it, as the living temple of God's light.

"Soon they will go forth, and it will begin. But they will not be separate from us. Although a body here and there might be a distance away, not we ... We are with them.

"Beyond the twilight of what lies ahead shall come a call. Open your hearts, open your spirits, to hear these words of truth: The call will be given seven times. Let your spirits remember this moment, for the calls shall be as seven golden steps, that each of us shall reclaim the beauty, the wonder, the preciousness, of the gift we bear.

"He will lead the way." Jacob points to the Master. "And it will appear that He has been forsaken. But in those moments of His journey, you will see in His eyes, as He will see in ours, that nothing can separate us.

"When the journey does resume and you hear the calls, take them within.

"Some of you will return," he gestures to the Maidens, "to help prepare the Way. Others of you will walk with them, just as the Ancient Ones walk with us now. And others of you will carry on and give the strength, the purity, and the beauty, which only you have to give. All are great in the sight of God. None is lesser. Howsoever the world beyond the twilight shall see you, heed not their illusion, but listen to that which speaks to you from within and from beyond.

"Come. We must depart." Jacob gestures to the Master who rises, pausing just a moment to glance about the group a final time. He strides directly to Jacob's side, to be embraced by his outstretched arm.

Jacob looks across the circle. "John, it is time."

John rises, looks about, nods, smiles, and gestures from his heart to each of the Maidens who in times past has held him as her own. He, too, then walks to Jacob's side to receive the embrace of his other arm.

"Celebrate," Jacob states firmly, looking at each one in the group. "Rejoice. It begins."

Without another word, the three turn and stride from the courtyard to the portal where Nicodemus stands holding the door awide. With silent prayers between them as they pass him by, they exit.

Several of the others rise to follow them. But Nicodemus closes the door and slowly shakes his head. They move with a heaviness back into the courtyard.

Several of the Maidens once again raise their hands and begin to clap and sing and dance their dance.

Anna emerges, steadied by two who are with her. "Jacob said, *Rejoice, Celebrate.* Can we do less than this?"

All rise and the celebration begins anew.

As we rise up through the courtyard and look down upon them, we turn to you, dear friends, and offer this from Jacob:

❧

The dawning is, indeed, here. We have passed beyond the twilight. We have journeyed through the darkness. And the Light emerges.

Will you hear its call? Will you look within and see that it is your name being called?

Shall you allow the call of Earth or limitation to take a greater position than the gift you have borne to this point?

Such a great journey, such wondrous opportunity is now before you.

∂∽ঔ

The only temple and teaching that can truly endure is that which is held within the mind and heart of the faithful. No matter how sound the structure built of earth or stone, it will pass away, but the temple within is eternal. It awaits you now.

Chapter Seven

Repent

The evening fire is small, but sufficient to illuminate the faces of those who are gathered around it. They are just a few paces from the Sacred Spring, and as they are seated about the small flame and its embers, we look upon their faces. Here we find Josie, Jessie, Moira, Anna, Judy, Zelotese, Marta, and Iliam.

"What works are taking place in the outer world at present?" Josie asks softly. "I so long for our Sisters' presence here. Perhaps they shall return soon, at least for a visit."

Anna, looking up at the evening sky, glances about, noting several other small flames a short distance away from theirs. Catching the attention and eye of Rebochien, she gestures to him.

He rises to walk over, and the group makes room for him to join them. He is followed by a number of others, and the circle grows in size and number.

"We were asking," returns Josie to her earlier question, "about the nature of activities in the outer world. Have you recent knowledge of these?" She leans to look at Rebochien.

"Ah, that I do. But, then, perhaps you as well know these things and greater." He nods at Iliam and several others. "For I note, brother Iliam, you are oft with John and about his works." Rebochien smiles broadly.

Iliam tilts his head and looks steadily at Rebochien and

laughs softly. "Well, it is difficult to be with John and not be around a lot of work."

The entire group laughs at this.

"He has them going about doing all manner of service."

"So we have heard," Anna interjects. "And much to the chagrin of those in authority. What do the Roman soldiers do in the presence of such works?"

"Nothing," Iliam looks down, his face more serious as he adds quietly, "as yet." Then he looks up and glances around the circle. "You know the truths of our teachings and you know the power that such truth, when intended from the Spirit and brought forth to meet a need from which there has been the request ... Well, it is no small matter. And even those in authority have come unto his followers ... I might better call them brothers and sisters, lest my word gets back to him and he chastise me for using it." Laughter echoes again. "But even several of the judges have sought him out. And I know personally of a temple priest who has come for assistance for some dis-ease. So, in brief, based on my experiences in the outer world, quite a bit is taking place."

The vast expanse of wilderness seems like a cloak embracing the solitary figure leaning over a small fire made to bring a bit of light, a bit of warmth, but too small to be seen at any distance.

In the periphery of the firelight, several creatures can be seen casually at rest, as though not even recognizing that a man is seated before the flame. Both flame and human alike are alien to them, yet they seemingly pay them no heed, eyes fluttering in semi-slumber, but, as so oft seen here, ever watchful over this one whom they appear to regard as unique.

John begins to rock ever so slightly and then he becomes still. As he peers at the evening sky, smiling as he looks upon its configurations, the image of Rebochien flashes in his memory. His hands extend towards the sky. With his right hand, the left still extended up, he strikes his chest thrice.

Rebochien stiffens and utters audibly.
They look at him.
"What troubles you, Rebochien?" questions Judy, scrutinizing him carefully. "I see a different light suddenly around you."
He reaches his hand up to rub his chest. "A sudden energy or something, as if something passed through me."
Judy nods. "I see it. It is a Light. Someone is remembering you in prayer, Rebochien."
"Oh, yes, I feel the power of it. Perhaps it is the Master remembering us."
Iliam, bent just slightly, also studies Rebochien, then breaks into a smile. "It is he of whom we have been speaking. There is no mistake of that light."
Rebochien smiles and strikes his chest thrice.

John raises his right hand again, smiling, for he knows his blessing has been received. He brings his hands down, resting them carefully in his lap. Moving just a bit, eyes closed as though he were peering through the eyelids themselves, his thoughts race across the barren waste of the wilderness beyond him, as a messenger of light soaring easily, rising up, the land below fading.

The essence of existence rushes against his consciousness. In this consciousness, he can perceive the glint of the starry night shimmering on waters below. There, a vessel is under sail, and towards its bow is a figure seated cross-legged. Looking out across the curvature of the bow's foremast is the Master, peering off into the distance.

A flush of light and energy passes through Him, and He smiles instantly. Straightening His garments and placing His folded hands upon His lap, He straightens Himself and turns His head upward. What light exists shines upon Him and we hear Him in the stillness. "I greet you, sweet brother. I am well, and I see and know that you are, as well, in goodness."

Perceiving this, John stirs. Pangs of emotion rush through him. He longs to touch this one again. Then he feels this:

"Be about Our Father's work, good brother. I know that thou art, but be of courage and faith. In a time ahead, I shall join you again. My blessings to you. And to all our brothers and sisters. Give them of Our Father's Light in the faith and courage that is our truth."

Rebochien shakes himself. His eyes blink several times.

Studying him, Iliam questions, "What else, brother?"

"The Master." Rebochien speaks softly and his head slumps forward.

The subtle light of the campfire catches the glint of several tears, as they fall to rest upon his knees.

They all bow their heads for a moment.

Anna offers this prayer: "Sweet Brother Yeshua, it is we, Thy brothers and sisters. Beloved brother John, here are we. We are one with you. May the Promise grow. May your journey be filled with the abundance of God's service, Brother. And unto thee, John, we give of our hearts and spirits that you might make the way ready for His return. Do so in good service and joy. The Peace of God be upon you both."

"Good sirs, please! Can you help me?" The man cries out, his body obviously in great pain. His twisted limbs struggle to find a position that will not wrack his body with the ravaging pain and dis-ease that has befallen him. A grimy hand is extended upward, fingers somewhat gnarled with the onset of the early stages of this dis-ease.

James is the first to stop. He turns and steps within a pace or two of the man who is lying against the wall, no more than twenty paces from the temple. Glancing about, he notes that his group is being observed by several of the Roman soldiers.

One of the soldiers contemplates for a moment whether or not to confront them, but chooses merely to observe them. He raises his hand to grasp the upper portion of his lance and rests his chin on it as though idle, yet his eyes, as James notes, are clearly fixed upon their small group.

Turning back to look at this one, who obviously has not much time left in this life's journey, James glances at Moira, then over to Thaddeus. He bends to a knee. "What seekest thou of us, good brother?" he asks gently.

"Please, I see that you are one of those who follow Him."

"What seest thou?" questions James.

"The lancets, and that which you have about your neck."

Glancing down, James realizes that the ornate pouch and its beautiful cord lie exposed on the outside of his garment. As casually as he can, so as to not arouse attention, he places it back inside, covering it somewhat while glancing over to his left at the Roman in the distance who is still watching them.

"Is it so? Art thou among His group?" the man persists.

"We are," James acknowledges softly.

Now Moira has come to kneel on both knees. "What is amiss for thee, good brother?"

Quickly he turns his head to see her. Only one eye functions well, for the other is crusted over. "I know of you. You have given unto others great healings. Please," he looks back at James, "could you ask your God to bring me either the peace of leaving this body or its restoration? In either case I shall joyfully repay in service whatsoever your God bestows upon me. I know you are with the Prophet. And I know your people do not perform such works unless asked, and so I do."

Moira has the palm of her hand upon his brow, brushing away fragments of dirt and debris, then runs its back down over his whiskery cheek. "You have fever," she comments.

The man merely looks at her, struggling to open both eyes, but cannot.

Reaching down, she pulls out a small skin and moistens a cloth that she removes from her outer garment. Quietly speaking some words that the man does not understand, she dabs the cloth gently over the eye that is swollen closed. His other eye closes in obvious gratitude.

Thaddeus, resting on one knee on the man's other side, reaches within his outer cloak and pulls forth several packets. Glancing about, he sees a young man, just a pace or so away. "You, there."

"I?"

"Yes. Will you earn several coins?"

"What must I do?"

"You must tend to this one."

"Why me?"

Thaddeus silently pulls forth several coins.

The young man's eyes open awide. "Tell me what I am to do."

Moira speaks softly. "Of these packets, make up a tea. Take them and …" She proceeds to instruct him about the amounts of herbs, when to administer them, and so forth.

"Here? In this square, with them watching?" The young man nods inconspicuously at several soldiers who are gathered across the way talking and laughing.

"With this coin secure lodging," Thaddeus instructs him. "And with this one, do your work. Go there," he points to a structure down at the end of the lane, "and secure lodging. Feed him. Nourish yourself and him, cleanse his body as my sister has instructed. Give him these herbs. In three days we shall return and if you have done these things, we will give you an equal amount of coins."

"In truth you speak?"

James looks at him, the fire in his eyes unmistakable.

The young man at first cowers at the sense of authority,

but then relaxes as James smiles.

"We speak truth … three days."

The man has managed to open his other eye ever so slightly and is already speaking words of praise and thanks.

"Gather him up now," James directs the young man, adding, "Here, take my staff, brother," as he hands it to the one who is diseased.

"I cannot accept this."

"You can. I will return for it in three days, and you can hand it to me … standing!"

"This will be true? Your God has told you?"

James smiles, looking down as the man's hand trembles to grasp this staff of one of the Prophet's healers.

"In the stillness of one's very soul there can always be found that which guides. Never is there the emptiness that others in the outer world seem to believe. So it is in the temple within that He will awaken them. I know this, Zephorah."

"But there must be more that we can be doing. Our brothers and sisters are out there, Hannah." She gestures off toward the horizon. "Why not we? Why do we remain here?"

"Let us ask, then, if we might also go forth and serve. I know all the reasons, the purposes for remaining here, but my spirit calls out unto me, *Hannah, go thou forth and serve. Answer those calls as there must be aplenty.*"

"There are, indeed, aplenty," Gideon interjects, having approached silently.

"Aye, that is so," Obadiah affirms.

Turning, Zephorah and Hannah see many guardians present here in the encampment all at one time, which brings great smiles of delight to them. They rise to embrace these warrior priests, offering words of love and gratitude for their dedication. "We are very pleased to have you with us. But unto what purpose are you here?"

A long pause follows. Finally, with his familiar smile, Nathanael the guardian responds, "You called us, did you not?"

Hannah's face flushes. "But I only spoke the words, if that is your meaning."

He leans on his great glistening staff. "Perhaps we heard your spirit calling before your words were spoken." He smiles, glancing at his brothers. "We are here for you. If you seek to serve in the outer world then we shall guide and protect you."

Zephorah, Hannah, and others of the Holy Maidens who have gathered to listen to what has transpired move swiftly to their elder sisters. A council is convened.

It is agreed that two by two they might go forth for a time, perhaps a fortnight, and then return, at which point the decision will be made as to how to proceed thereafter.

In a muted, sweet voice Judy assents. "Go forth, then, sweet sister Hannah. And who with you?"

Instantly Rebekah raises her hand, and she and Hannah excitedly reach out to embrace one another.

"Very good. Gideon, watch over them."

"I will, too, dear Judy." Nathanael looks down at these two sweet Sisters. "For there are two of them and they have quite a history of being, shall I call it, active. It might be more than my brother can deal with, for there are times, you know, when even we do sleep."

They all laugh.

It is near twilight and the main gate to Jerusalem is about to be closed. Several of the guards on the exterior step forward, looking at the small group moving towards the gate.

"You, there! No more are to enter this eve. Seek you encampment yonder. At sunrise we shall reopen the city. No more. Be gone."

Nathanael, wearing the outer garments of a typical trader,

begins to take a step forward.

But Hannah raises an arm and calls out, "Thank you, good sir, we shall find encampment where you have directed, and return on the morrow."

Glancing at the guard, most of his face covered, Nathanael momentarily makes eye contact with him, and the guard feels a rush of something. "Have I seen you in the past, traveler?" he inquires warily, his lance now tipped somewhat ominously forward.

The other guard, noting this, does the same, and they begin to walk towards Nathanael and the others.

"That would be very unlikely. We are from Tyre, and have not journeyed here before. We have come to visit a friend who is in service to the court and has recently taken lodging here."

"Name him," the first guard demands, approaching even closer.

"He is called Nicodemus."

The guard stops, glances at the other, and then resting his lance upon the ground again, states in a surly tone, "Very well. I know of him. Go to the encampment. I shall look upon you in the dawn's light." He looks at Nathanael sternly. "And if I recall you from the past, you will answer my questions."

They have settled in, silently joined together in their prayers, and taken the teas and herbs that preserve them from all manners of dis-ease, as is the custom among their people.

"Knowest thou him?" Rebekah questions Nathanael.

Uncovering his head and face, Nathanael glances at Gideon and receives a powerful look in response. "That we do," he admits quietly. "He was among those who pursued our peoples with that captain, so long ago. Indeed, sweet Sisters, he sought to take your very lives."

Hannah's hands come up to cover her face, and she begins to weep as she recalls those sweet guardians who gave all to preserve their lives as they fled into the wilderness to the shelter of the great School.

"You still remember?" Gideon questions gently.

"Yes, my spirit remembers all. My mind cannot envision it all, but my spirit tells me. Let us offer prayer for our brethren who gave that which they had to give that the Promise might endure."

At dawn's light they come not by that same gate, but one beyond, and enter unobtrusively. The same guard wanders around the encampment with several of his colleagues, looking, searching. Finally, he stops to turn to his comrades. "Well, one of two things has happened; they have come into the city by the east gate, or they have departed. I shall ask the captain's permission to seek within the city. I would know of what I recall. I have the sense that he is one of the rebels."

Several of the other guards look at each other quickly. "What can it mean?"

"I do not know, but I intend to find out."

"Shall we go seek Nicodemus?" Hannah asks softly.

"No, let us go beyond it. Let us visit the abode of James and John."

"Zebedee?"

"Yes," Nathanael responds. "If that guard recalls what I do, they will be searching."

"Oh!" Rebekah looks down as they walk. "What an un-fortunate entry. Perhaps we should leave while we can."

Gideon glances at Nathanael. "No, we came for a pur-pose, else your spirits would not have called out. Let us be about that work. Surely it is that intended by God, and, therefore, the power, the Spirit of God, is with us."

The warm embraces and the serving of food are followed

by conversations among James, John, and the group.

"Where are your parents?" Rebekah questions.

"They are away," James begins quietly. "They have gone to visit our uncle and shall return, perhaps, in several days. If you remain, surely you will see them. I know they will be overjoyed to see you again."

Gideon appears at the entryway. "My brother and I shall depart now. But fear not. You perhaps will not see us, but we shall still be keeping watch over you all, nonetheless."

Hannah and Rebekah rise to embrace these sweet brothers, who smile as they glance back and slip away into the lane before this house.

"Where do you suppose they will go?" Rebekah asks.

"I know not, but as you well know, they will not be found. Of that, I am certain."

Ascending several inclines and moving around the structure that is before them, the guardians come to rest at a high place where the juncture of several walls comes together. As they seat themselves and bring out skins and foodstuffs from beneath their outer garments, Nathanael gazes around at the sprawl of the rooftops and whispers, "One wonders why they live like this."

Without acknowledging his brother's gaze and gesture, Gideon looks instead at some morsels of bread and cheese. "Each must answer unto their own calling, I suppose." He looks up, handing a bit of foodstuffs to Nathanael, who accepts them with a gesture of prayer.

"When He comes I wonder if any of this will change."

"Doubtful," Gideon responds reflectively. "The Ancient Ones told us it will likely take considerable time before the truth of His words and teachings resonates and comes to rest within those who are seeking."

"Why sayest thou unto us, *Repent*? Who art thou to

speak such words?" demands a tall, well-dressed member of the group before John.

"Must I be of some stature to speak truth to you, sir?"

"Thou speakest with authority," the tall one objects, his face twisted in a spiteful attitude.

Paying no mind to this, John slips down to rest on a slight outcropping of the rock and soil behind him. "If I speak to you with authority and tell you of the nature of that office, will you the moreso consider what I say as truth?"

"Of course." He turns to look at the others in the group and gestures. "We all would."

"Really?" John slowly smiles, his head tilted to the side. "And you there. Would you trust my words the better, if I tell you of a certain office that I hold?"

A small, slight maiden looks all around to be certain that John is speaking to her, then looks down and back up at him. "No, I know of you. I have seen your works and the works of those who are with you. Thou art a messenger of God."

"A what?" questions the tall, well-dressed one.

"In truth, he is." Several other maidens step around to stand by her and echo her words.

"Words are easily come by," the well-dressed one retorts. "Give me an action that will tell me that thou hast authority," he demands.

"Oh, very well," John replies, almost casually. He stands, reaching out to grasp a staff lying off to the side. "Come forth, friend."

"You come to me."

"I will tell you what … I will come to you, but not in this body. I will come to you inside you."

"Impossible!"

"Is it?" John is now leaning upon his staff. "I will come to you, within you, in this way." John's eyelids flutter for just a few brief moments.

The small woman standing over to the side, having seen

this previously on a number of occasions, brings her hands up in silent prayer.

John looks away towards the slope leading to the water at the river's edge, and then extends his right hand and arm, the forefinger pointing directly at the affluent one. "Thou art a merchant, as I see within thee. Thou art in command of several, shall I call them, trading places." John turns to glance sharply at him.

The merchant, a bit uneasy, quickly regains his composure. "Anyone could know that. And I do not feel a thing within me, as you said."

Smiling, John looks down his arm playfully, as though he were sighting down a weapon, but, of course, it is merely his forefinger. "I see that your merchandise lives. I see that you trade in human life. And I see that you are damned!"

The man's face pales.

"I see that recently you have gathered several off the streets who were orphaned, and against their will you have sold them into bondage. So I say to you, *Repent!* For that which is within you is that which you shall become. Whatsoever you do unto a brother or a sister will return unto you. And when the Prophet cometh, He will say this to you in the Voice of God. What say you, merchant?"

The merchant pales even more and steps back, somewhat concerned that some in this group might seek to retaliate.

There is a stirring, as several large, surly-looking males come forward. They are clearly part of the rebellion and are working their way through the group, as the merchant can clearly see.

John turns to face them and raises his hand. "Hold your wrath. It is not for you to judge this one, but for him to judge himself, and in the doing of such, to discover that which is awry and bring it into righteousness. Look you, merchant, your hand is withering before your eyes. For it doeth this work of bondage against your own peoples."

Regaining his composure at the halting of the surly renegades, the merchant turns to look defiantly at John. "Here are my hands, thou false prophet, see them?" turning them front and back. "They are whole and perfect, and, I might add, somewhat cleaner than yours."

"Is it so?" questions John softly. "Look you carefully upon the right. For it has done the work and received the coin. Look upon it carefully. Look at the back of it. There you will see the mark of each soul you have placed into bondage."

The merchant cannot resist looking at his own hand. At first there is nothing, and he smirks and spits out words of retaliation.

Then, someone standing to his right staring intently at the merchant's upraised hand gasps. "Look, a dark area!"

Fuming, the merchant turns to look at him, but as he gazes back at his own hand, he, too, gasps aloud.

"And another, and another! He has the plague!"

The others fall away, moving backwards away from the merchant. Just as he had stood in authority, he now stands alone.

John, peacefully gazing at the merchant, says nothing.

As his hand darkens more and more, the merchant begins to curse aloud. He brings his hand down and shakes it, rubs it, removes a fine embroidered cloth from within his garment and rubs his hand briskly. "Thou art a sorcerer, not a prophet of God. Thou hast cast a spell, and I believe it not. My will is the greater than yours."

"It is not my will, but the Will of God in the truth of His Law: *As ye have wrought, so is it given unto thee.* I have merely asked that the Law surround and bless thee according to its truth."

"How can you ask such a thing, and of whom do you ask it?" The merchant looks around, continuing to rub his hand vigorously.

"I ask of the One God, and I ask in the name of that

which is truth. And I call upon the Law to bless you. The Law, being perfect, will bring unto you whatever you have sown to be your harvest, now."

"How can you command such a harvest to befall me now in a certain time and place?"

Striding slowly, not even looking at him any longer, John walks down the hill toward the river's edge. "Because I believe unto it." He glances sharply back up at the merchant.

Such light and fire shine in John's eyes that the merchant recoils. His hand is beginning to wither, his fingers are becoming swollen and gnarled. He begins to cry out in pain and fear, cursing John and cursing that unto which he calls.

John, not minding him, but hearing his words, speaks loudly without looking at him. "If thou repent, then thy sins can be forgiven thee, good merchant. It is your choice. And now is the time to make it."

Standing knee-depth in the river, John leans on his staff. With remarkable serenity on his face, he turns to the merchant. "Seek ye to repent, friend? Or shall that which you have sown continue to be harvested?"

The crippling effect on his hand is moving up his arm, which is now twisted. The merchant falls to his knees, weeping, rubbing it. "I curse you this day, thou sorcerer, and all that thou art about! I have no need of thee. I will see the physicians in the city. They shall take this curse from me and bring it back unto you!" He stumbles to his feet and begins to move away.

We see John bow his head in prayer, asking God for forgiveness of a brother gone astray.

Hannah and Rebekah stroll through the city streets, somewhat awestruck by what they see. Foul smells and odors of all kinds fill the spaces between the crowded structures on either side. The Maidens take great care where they walk, for beneath their feet is the litter of many, many peoples of many years. Looking into this opening and that, they see small groups gathered intermittently. For the most part, they have moderate belongings, but on occasion the Maidens come to one or another entry that is decorated, even somewhat re-splendent. As they progress upwards towards the temple, the structures become ever more beautiful.

"The greater one's stature in this community," James clarifies, "the closer one lives to the temple."

"Is it a question of wealth?" Rebekah asks.

"It is that and position. These two things are essentially inseparable."

"And their trade," John interjects. "Those who have something that those of highest authority desire are brought closer to the authorities and to the temple itself."

"Goodness. And what of all the others below, and in the other lanes?"

"For the most part," John answers, "they do what they can to survive; you know, the things that those with power will not do for themselves. These people ..." He turns to gesture with a sweeping hand at the rooftops sprawled out below them. "These people do those things."

Hannah and Rebekah glance at one another and continue their journey, questioning, seeking.

Off in the shadows some distance behind, heavily cov-ered with outer garments and stooped over as though they are elderly, come Gideon and Nathanael. They speak rarely, only when need be, and now pause in a corner alcove at a square where they can see their brothers and sisters very clearly.

Towards the left, a loud commotion erupts. A man dressed in finery comes running into the square, waving a withered hand and arm upward. "Sorcerer! Devil's work! Look you. I call upon those of authority. Seek him out and destroy him, lest he do this to you as well."

The group into which he has rushed quickly moves away,

for it could be the sickness. Glancing at one another, they slowly begin to move to where the merchant has seated himself on the circular stone bench surrounding the pool in the square.

Splashing water from the pool onto his hand and arm, the merchant cries out in a mixture of weeping and cursing.

Irresistibly drawn, they move closer.

Finally Hannah steps forward and asks, "Forgive us, good sir, but we have heard your words. Of whom do you speak, that has so cursed you?" She looks down with concern at his hand, now very discolored and gnarled.

As the merchant slips off his outer cloak, she gasps as she sees that the dis-ease is progressing up his arm. He slumps over and places his decaying arm on the edge of the city pool and begins to weep. "It is the one in the wilderness."

"He cursed you?" questions Hannah gently.

Glancing up defiantly, the merchant responds. "He did. Have you not eyes to see my hand and arm? This is his work," waving it in front of Hannah and Rebekah, who has come to stand at Hannah's side.

"Why would he do this to you?" Rebekah asks softly.

By this time several others have gathered a safe distance away. Among the group is a slight young maiden who, surprisingly, speaks out. "He did naught to the merchant," she offers in a clear, sweet voice. "He called upon God to bring this one unto justice," pointing at him. "We knew he would come here and seek revenge for that one in the wilderness, and so we are come to bring the other side of the story to those who might seek to harm this worker in God's Name."

The merchant has now placed his good arm on the stone wall around the well and is weeping. With tear-filled eyes, he looks up, and speaking directly to Hannah, James, his brother John, and Rebekah, he spews, "Is what I have done so wrong that this one in the wilderness would call upon my past to visit this hand and arm?"

"What is it that is your labor?" James asks quietly.

"I am a merchant. That is all."

"And what is your merchandise?" questions John.

His demeanor softening, the merchant turns to look at him and answers, for the first time, in a voice that is open. "I trade in servants, nothing more. I do not harm them. In fact, I ofttimes bring them into better health and certainly better cleanliness and garb."

"And your intent in so doing?" Hannah presses gently.

"That they would bring greater coin, of course."

"So you actually sell them into service to others?"

"Many do this. Why not I?"

"Then this is what he has called up to visit upon you," James responds. "Not that which he has called forth to curse you, but to call out that which is of goodness within you."

The merchant is weeping again. "How do I find such goodness?"

"Thou wouldst go unto that which thou hast wrought, and make it aright," Hannah offers.

"Indeed." Rebekah adds. "Whatsoever you have gained upon the loss of another must be balanced."

The merchant snaps. "How can I do this? You mean go purchase them back?"

"Yes," Hannah answers simply. "And unto them give what you, yourself have … freedom. And of that which you have to give, give a measure unto each. That is the goodness that the one in the wilderness is seeking to call forth."

The pain in his arm has moved to the shoulder and he grimaces, wailing aloud.

Many on the periphery have stopped to watch this scene, and several of the Romans have moved closer.

Gideon has moved to the opposite side of the square and Nathanael has found shelter at the entry gate to the west, their eyes catching every movement, observing.

Fortunately, the guards in authority this day have better

things to do. Several are laughing and talking with a young maiden, two more up the way towards the temple are imbibing wine and foodstuffs, and are also laughing. Occasionally glancing to see who it is that cries out and satisfied that there is no challenge, no discord of note, the guards return to their activities.

The merchant is bent over with pain. Obviously, the effects of the deeds he has willfully performed in the past are manifesting fruits now in that which he suffers. "I will do it. No more!" he whimpers. "Please, can you ask him to take the curse from me?"

"Where is he?" Hannah asks the young maiden across the breadth of the well.

She gestures with an outstretched arm. "At the river's edge."

"Come, merchant. If your promise is true in your heart, you can be free of your pain."

They help the stumbling merchant, and, ultimately, along with the young maiden who has spoken out on John's behalf, they find a goodly number gathered at the river's edge. As they make their way down to the bank of the water, they hear the clear voice of one standing in it, calling out unto God again and again. They hear his voice singing praise unto God and blessing and embracing each one who has come forth in repentance, seeking His goodness.

A great smile flashes across John's face as he sees his brothers and sisters. He embraces each of them with his eyes, but only briefly, for the work is before him.

The merchant is now upon his knees, his good hand covering his eyes as he weeps.

John walks slowly out of the water and extends his hand. "Come thou, brother. Come."

Unable to speak, able only to weep, the merchant stumbles forward. As John kneels in the water at its edge, the merchant does the same.

Cupping the river water, John holds it up. "Look you, good brother: The true Spirit of Life. As it courses through here and along the banks of this river's edge, so does it course within you. With it within, you can bring forgiveness, just as I, son of God, now offer this forgiveness to you."

From a bowl that he has taken from beneath his garment, he pours water over the merchant's bowed head. His tears and the water from John's bowl intermingle, as the reflected light present, which is just a few hours before twilight, glistens on the droplets as they fall back into the river.

"Look, my brother. Thy sins depart thee. Wash them away from within, just as God now washes them away from without."

The merchant begins to cough and sputter.

John continues to offer blessings to him whom he now calls his brother. Reaching around and replacing the bowl beneath his garment, John places his right hand on the man's withered shoulder. "In the name of the Holy One, the Christ, do I now bless thee. Thy sins are forgiven thee."

There is absolute silence.

Gasping follows as the merchant begins to straighten himself. As if he were a newborn, his arm begins to thrash about, splashing on the water's surface. His face beams with Light as he brings his hand up, no longer withered or dark- ened. Turning it over and back, then looking up at John, he asks, "Have I come from a dream? Has this been naught but within me?"

John smiles down at him. "Thou knowest the truth. But that which is whole on the outer must be made whole on the inner. You must go forth and make righteous that which you, as you adjudge it, have done in error, or against another. Hear my words well, O brother. If you do not do this in a fortnight, that which is sown will be harvested again, and not I can make it aright. Only He who bears the Promise, the Light of God, could do such. And He is not at hand, save in His Spirit in the words I have given you."

Jumping to his feet, the merchant rushes out of the water and having gone a good number of paces, turns and looks back. "Thou art a prophet. Thou art a messenger of God. And I hear your words within."

Turning to look at Hannah and Rebekah, he steps forward and reaches out his hands, one to each of them, and they clasp his. He bends to kiss each Maiden's hand. "I give the thanks of my heart and spirit to you, good maidens," he says, looking at them carefully. Glancing at James and John, the merchant adds, "And brothers, thank you for bringing me to this Light." He looks back at John who's already busy speaking with the others in the water.

"I would that you remember me." He gazes deeply into Hannah's and Rebekah's eyes. "I am called Levites. I am ever at your service. I go now to right that which I have wronged." He takes a few strides and turns to look back. "When I have finished this work and made all aright, I will return to serve with him," gesturing towards John in the water. "And I shall ask that God give me new birth and perhaps even a new name that might bear honor to what I shall intend to do with him, and perhaps you as well. I know not what you hold as secrets in your hearts and spirits, all of you. But I have tasted of the cup of your goodness. I wish to be one with it." He turns and strides briskly back towards the city.

Such a cup is within each of you, dear friends, the one that holds only the goodness of God. As you seek within, you can find many cups that hold many differing potentials for you in your journey through life. But upon journey's end, this is that cup which endureth beyond all else.

To the measure you have taken of it and given of it, it shall be that cup which shall sustain thee into the Kingdom of our Father.

Chapter Eight

Journeying Eastward

As though gazing into the campfire will force something to speak to them, long pauses pass between the comments bantered back and forth in this small group. Their obvious disagreement is unlike these beautiful peoples. Although they have separated from the family, the tribe in the area of the Three Holy Mountains, nonetheless, their hearts and spirits are ever one with them.

One looks up from the fire into the eyes of Moesha. "I disagree with you. I believe that the further we move into the wilderness, into its distant remote areas, the more vulnerable we will become."

"How so?"

"I feel that the closer we are in proximity to settlements and villages and towns, the easier it is for us to be less noticeable, less conspicuous. There is some degree of safety in numbers. Here," gesturing with his hand outward, "there is nothing but us. No one else seeks to dwell in these lands. So, in my humble opinion and according to my guidance, we should return north and find suitable quarters on the fringes of, if not overly near the settlements there."

After another long pause, Moesha insists gently, "I tell you again, no good shall come from all of this. The Forerunner should not be speaking and acting as he is, and neither should the others, in my humble opinion. I believe we are righteous in our movement. And while I welcome and thank you for your comments and your guidance, I must stand with the previous decisions."

His eyes struggle to flicker open, as though something were opposing his will and striving to hold them closed. Slowly he begins to see the mid-morning light. Unaware of where he is in terms of consciousness or physical locale, he glances about, striving to find something familiar.

He feels a sharp pain and glances down. A sizable wound gapes in his lower right abdomen. Slowly bringing his hand up, and a bit of his outer coat as well, he covers the wound and applies pressure to it. With great effort, gasping and sucking in his breath, Raphael raises himself on one elbow.

Boulders bar his field of vision somewhat, as a great whirlwind of realization reminds him that this is where he had fallen during last night's battle. Wisps of smoke rise here and there, bodies are strewn this way and that. No familiar cookfires blaze. Only a few moans, that is all.

Dizzied by what he beholds, he falls backward and lies motionless, looking up into the mid-morning sky. Several large clouds drift lazily by as though not beholding not what has befallen his tribe.

He looks to his right and sees the dark earthen color of the rocks, then to his left, and realizes that he has fallen into a small crevice that no doubt shields him from those who would silence utterly what they believe to be the voices of the Zealots.

His head spins as thoughts flee in and out of his consciousness, echoes of discussions of not that long ago about where these, his beloved peoples, should take shelter and call home. He thinks of his brothers, the other guardians to the south, for whom he feels great love and oneness. As he does, he strives to hold the image of several of them. *To what avail?* his mind cries. Yet his spirit reaches out, trying to grasp a hand of light that might be extended by a brother's spirit ... distant, yet always close in heart.

A small scraping, shuffling sound stirs Raphael back to consciousness. Again he rises slowly and painfully on one elbow, noting wounds and bruises on his hand and arm. Yet they support him by his use of sheer will or intent.

Beautiful soft brown eyes, tears flowing, suddenly connect with his.

Raphael sighs deeply. "Are there others?"

Her voice cracks. "A few, a very few."

He strives to sit up, but winces, and an uncontrollable moan escapes him.

"Here, let me help you." She moves to the side and slips through the narrow entryway between the obstructing rocks and the side of the cliff. Bending, she reaches within her outer cloak and pulls forth several small containers of herbs. From the other side she brings out a skin of water. Moistening a strip of material torn from her coat, she carefully sprinkles the odd powders and fragments of leaves into its fold.

Studying her, Raphael smiles. *It could have been she,* he thinks. *She could have brought the Promise into the Earth, and it might have been she and our people who would have embraced and nurtured the Promise.* He surprises himself with an audible sigh.

Quickly her eyes dance upward to meet his, their softness seeming to caress him with her sweetness and love. "Raphael, what is your intent?"

His eyes flicker and a smile flashes on his face, "You mean, do I intend to depart or remain?"

For a moment, her face softens sweetly, and she laughs a little dancing rivulet of laughter. "That is what I mean."

"Well," he shifts his body, "God willing, and this temple of flesh support me, I choose to remain."

Rachael sighs deeply. She tenderly places the poultice over the wound, having rinsed it first with the water. "Put pressure on this." She looks at him sternly. "And keep it there until I can find binding for you. Can you rise?"

"I am not sure. I will try." He struggles this way and that, pulling his large frame free from its previous resting place amid the smaller rocks in the crevice. On one foot and struggling to apply pressure, he lifts his great frame as Rachel tries to support him as best her small frame can manage. Once on his feet, he hobbles out with her through the opening by which she had come to find him.

With one arm about Rachel's shoulders, all but eclipsing her from view, he strikes his chest with his left hand. "Holy Father, grant them peace," he prays, as he looks about and surveys the destruction and desolation of what one short day ago had been their comfortable little village and settlement. "The children, where are the children?" he asks.

"They have fled to the south, others of your brothers guarding them."

"To what destination?"

"I believe the lands of the Egyptians."

His head slumps. For with these words, he hears that the future of this, his people, is no more as he has known it, and that mayhaps he shall see those sweet brothers no more in this life. "And the Romans?"

"Gone," she answers dryly. "Obviously," she looks about, "there is nothing more here for them to do. Raphael, I must tell you, though, ..." She rubs her head where a great bruise is evident and small globs of blood mingle with her glistening auburn hair.

"Let me see that."

"No, no. I have treated it and it is subsiding. But listen, I heard their captain say that he has knowledge of our other families and their locale! And they intend ... Well, you can see." She sweeps her arm about. "How can we warn them?"

In great pain, Raphael comes to rest against an out-cropping. His head spinning, he mutters, "This I do not know."

The clanking of their crude armor and weapons against their shields seems intentional, as though to announce to those ahead of them on their pathway, *Here cometh authority. Bow your heads. Fall to your knees. We rule you.*

The file of soldiers marches, led by several in finery on horseback. Several more mounted warriors are on the flanks and a handful more to the rear, making certain that none of the captives escape.

Someone bursts into the doorway unannounced and un-invited. Those within jump to their feet, startled. James reaches beneath his outer coat for a small sword hidden behind the folds.

"Stay your hands," Thaddeus announces boldly, "and forgive me. It is I, your brother." He turns to close the door, but first looks up and down the street. Seeing naught, he enters and stumbles exhausted to the fireside.

"Here," James urges. "Drink this brew. You look absolutely worn out."

Head bowed, shoulders hunched, Thaddeus looks down at the fire, accepting the bowl of warm tea, brewed with the herbs and spices customary to the House of Zebedee.

John has moved a small stool over to where Thaddeus is now resting. Moira, Jessie, Hannah, Rebekah, and many of the other maidens who have gathered for the evening's meal and prayer on this Sabbath simply cover themselves as is their custom, arms folded, hands together, looking down. For they intuit that all is not well.

Rubbing his face, Thaddeus hands the bowl back to James.

John asks tenderly, "Please, speak to us Thaddeus if you are able to do so. What news have you?"

Swallowing hard, Thaddeus looks up, his eyes darting from one pair of eyes to the next and the next, awide with apprehension. He looks down for a moment, resting the palm of his right hand upon his heart. Without a thought or a word, the sisters all do the same.

James comes to rest on his heels before Thaddeus, and puts a hand on his shoulder. "All is within God's plan. All is according to that which is offered unto us. Remember, good brother, He would say unto you, *Thy strength lies within. That which is without, thy body, is the instrument. No matter what shall befall the instrument, the light of the Truth of God within us is eternal.*"

Thaddeus reaches up to put his other hand on James', still resting on his shoulder. As though drawing some strength through their eye contact, Thaddeus remains transfixed by James' open, welcoming gaze. "They are gone. Our family of Tyre is gone, save the children, who have fled to the Egyptian lands I am told."

Total silence.

Then softly, sweetly we can hear Hannah and Rebekah, who, kneeling, have turned to face each other, hands joined, foreheads touching, softly chanting words of prayer.

After a while, as the details unfold, Thaddeus adds, "And we have heard that the Romans march to the north. I have learned that one of our other families has been taken captive already and that even now as I speak to you, they are being brought here to be sold."

"What is their intent? Why are they doing this?"

"They believe, or perhaps have been told by some of the priests or elders who feel the Promise threatens them, that we are rebels, zealots, and that we are massing and making weaponry and whatnot. And that we intend to challenge them through deception, subterfuge, and worse!"

John and James exchange glances. Moira has come to seat herself, as has Jessie, among the men.

"What can we do?" Moira asks sweetly.

"Our prayers, of course," Thaddeus answers, as the two embrace each other visually.

"Is there naught we can do physically?" Jessie urges.

"It is too soon to know how to answer that," Thaddeus responds. "Some of this is only rumor, albeit from their messengers established to communicate rapidly between their holdings."

Only the barely audible sound of footsteps can be heard in the stillness. Against the backdrop of a moonless night, here and there a star points a finger of light over the form of one who is treading through the wilderness straight away, with long, bold strides towards the encampment.

Reaching his destination, John sucks in his breath, as did Raphael not long prior when he, too, eyed the desolation.

John sees a small flame, barely sufficient for a bit of light and cooking. The fire is glowing over in the far corner of a little depression that had been one of his family's homes. He can see several figures moving ever so slightly, carefully, in the shadows of its light.

Struggling to arm himself, Raphael stumbles forward, a staff held in the defensive position in front of him.

"Lay aside your arms, Raphael. It is I, John."

For a moment Raphael stands as though suspended in time. As he leans to brace himself on it, his stout staff makes a curious clanking sound as it strikes the rocks on the ground.

Without pausing, John strides directly up to Raphael and, having observed his condition, gently embraces him.

They rest their faces on one another's shoulders. Raphael weeps quietly.

Finally, John releases Raphael from his embrace. Keeping his hands upon Raphael's shoulders, he gazes into his eyes, understanding his sorrow. "It is the will of God," John whispers. "All of us shall cross through the Veil of Separation between this world and the next, each in our time, and each in service to the Promise."

Raphael, with a moment of doubt quite unlike him and

the other guardians, answers quietly but firmly, motioning with his head. "And what will was served by all this?"

Looking around, John sees the lifeless bodies, the devastation, the sacred writings burned, structures, everything gone, ruined, destroyed. He turns back to fix his eyes on Raphael's without a flicker of question or doubt in them.

Raphael sees this, and seems to draw a renewal of his own faith and strength from it.

"The work is before us," John asserts calmly. "All of these," glancing left and right, indicating with tilts of his head, "have given all they had to give, that that work shall be fulfilled. I say to you my sweet brother, Raphael, named after that one of justice and strength ... Be thou as that Angel of God. Summon thy strength that the temple of thy spirit's works, this temple of flesh," squeezing Raphael's shoulder as he speaks, "be whole. But more than this, let the Promise be whole within you, and let it shine forth as is righteous."

After a few wordless moments, Raphael finally evidences a small smile, and then a grin. "Come." He places an arm around John's shoulder. "Come, I forgot my manners, my teaching. We must give you nourishment."

Raphael cannot see this, but as they walk slowly, painfully on his part, towards the small fire, John's head slumps forward in silent prayer.

"What say these people, the Greeks, about the Promise forthcoming?"

"Those that we have made contact with and are a part of our journey are hopeful. They would welcome you joyfully."

"And this place where we shall lodge this evening, who is its master?"

"Galis is his name, and he is of high stature here in Greek society, some sort of a lawmaker or judge, from what I am told. But our other brethren who established friendships along our route to the East long ago can tell you more."

"Galis ... It is a name of strength and faith, so I feel," the Master observes quietly.

They are admitted into the House of Galis. Several of the Essenes who always precede the Master and the others are standing by Galis as he welcomes them. There follows the traditional greeting and welcoming according to Greek custom, and He is given all things unto His needs.

Having completed His prayer, meditation, and similar works, the Master is now seated, looking about the sumptuous surroundings of this abode.

Galis is seated across from Him. "May I come closer so I may speak with you?"

"Indeed." Jesus gestures casually to a seat close by Him to the left, facing the firestone hearth on the opposite wall, where a great fire is burning. Candles are everywhere. Such brightness indoors is not often beheld by these peoples.

"Are you the One of whom they speak and have foretold?"

"I am that which is here in your abode as a servant of God," the Master smiles gently. Seeing Galis' face betray indecision, the Master reaches across and bends slightly to touch him. "Speak what is in your heart, my friend."

Galis looks into the Master's eyes. "It is grievous to me to speak these words, for I dishonor myself and this house to speak such that would ask of you when you are here in my hospitality. Please forgive me."

The Master nods and responds softly, "That which is in your heart and mind is sweet, brother. Speak it."

"My daughter. Her condition is grave. If you are that One of whom they have spoken, can you ..."

"Of course," the Master answers gently, His demeanor unchanged. "Bring her to me."

Galis jumps to his feet and rushes out clapping his hands. Servants scurry, and a moveable bed is brought in. The furnishings are moved, and Galis' daughter is placed before the Master who has not moved, but simply leans to one side, an elbow on His leg.

The Master looks up at Galis. "What do you call her?"

"I call her Leah."

"Ah. It is after the flowers afield and the creatures that fly among them that your people bestow this name, true?"

Galis is surprised that one from such a far place would know this. He smiles and nods.

"And she has been this way long?" The Master now has risen. Standing over Leah, He smiles down, His hands clasped humbly together.

"Yes, a very long time, and she can no longer speak; nor does she acknowledge much of anything. She barely swallows to take fluids or foods."

Moving to Leah's head, the Master kneels upon His right knee, His right arm arched above her head. "Thou sweet child of God, I call thee Leah, but my Father has for thee many names. Hear thou my voice and my word. Come thou forth unto this world to those whose love awaits thee. Thy journey is not complete. In the Word and Law of God, I call thee forth." He places His right palm upon her forehead. "Leah, come thou forth."

The Master's eyes flicker but a moment or two. A shudder of something appears to pass through His body ever so briefly, visible, though, to the other Expectant Ones and the guardians who journey with Him.

With a gentle fluid motion of a bird in flight, the Master lifts His hand and places it over His heart, rises from His kneeling position, then turns and nods to one of the guardians standing off to the side.

With that, the guardians move into the chamber intended to honor the Master for His rest and needs.

Galis looks up wistfully, as they depart through this grand room and down a corridor. For a moment his thoughts race, *It can't be. One such as this, though He has a certain charm, a certain light, how could He be the Messiah, their so-called Promise? How …*

His musing is interrupted by a low, soft sound. His head snaps around as though some unseen force utterly possessed his body.

Her long eyelashes flutter. A pastel rosy color seems to be flushing her cheeks, which have been pale and ashen for so long. Then she smiles, and we hear, "Papa!"

When is He coming to our vessel?" the captain growls at the Essene before him.

"Soon. You have been reimbursed for your time and well paid for this journey."

"That is so, but I am the captain of this vessel. And look!" He points to the rolling clouds on the distant horizon. "It may be days before I can set sail if He doesn't come today! I tell you, I shall tell my men to seek shelter and do as they would for at least several days, if He does not arrive today."

"So be it then," the Essene responds with a gentle smile.

Stomping around, the captain moves to the upper portion of the stern and, opening a small door, enters the chamber there.

"I do not like his tone very much."

The other Essene shrugs his shoulders, responding quietly with a big smile. "I tell you, he is the best of the whole lot. The others are worse than that."

His brother shakes his head in disbelief. "What a way to live. All these years that we have been here in these lands." He gestures to the sprawl of structures haphazardly built as though someone took a large container of them and shook it, spilling them out all over the area.

"Well, such as it is, it is their choice, is it not?"

The second Essene sighs deeply as they turn to debark, moving down the gangway and back onto the land. They disappear in the maze of corridors and passageways that make up the waterfront area.

The sweet metallic sounds of the temple gongs and chimes seem to weave themselves into the fragrance of the sacred herbs and spices that continually and aromatically burn in small, scattered containers. Beautiful carvings and gilded idols stand here and there, not ominous, but warm, cheerful, invoking a sense of peace and tranquility, a sense of wellness.

The lama has been rocking and chanting in a soothing singsong voice. Those with him, his aides, his workers, seers, and such, are gaily bedecked.

We hear the soft shuffling of the monks who are guiding Him into this holy temple. Finally, they appear, wearing their beautiful scarlet garments that flow gently, almost wistfully, as though some life is present within the very fabric itself.

The lama rises, takes several steps forward, and bows. Those with him do likewise.

In the midst of the Essenes, following several guardians, the Master can be seen. As is the tradition of the Expectant Ones, He is freshly groomed and attired in a seamless garment, heavy, thick, yet subtle to the touch, coarse, yet comfortable to the skin on which it rests. The Master gestures, and places His hands on His heart. To the surprise of the Essenes accompanying Him, He then brings His hands together, first over the center of His being and out, as though to salute this Holy One, and then on upwards over His body.

The lama and his aides study this One who is come from so far away. The lama breaks into a warm smile and responds quickly, as do all the others, saluting the Master in word and gesture.

Having been afforded great comforts and wonderfully aromatic and tasty foods unlike any they, the Expectant Ones, have known (except for those who have resided here to prepare the way), they comment to this effect regarding the herbs and teas.

Several aides of the Holy One come forth with bundles and announce, "These are our gifts to you and your peoples. Take them and remember us, as you sip the brew made from them."

The Master nods and, without turning, lifts His right hand. One of the guardians steps forward and places a beautiful garment thereon. The Master extends it to the Holy One. "This is a gift from our people to you and your people. You would honor us, and our God, if you would accept it. This garment has been woven by the hands of those who among our people are holy. Twelve in all have touched it with love and compassion, and have placed their prayers and their salutations unto you within it. Each one has carefully and lovingly prepared the flax for it and has softened it with her hands and woven it with her spirit."

Turning it a bit He continues. "If you will note here, one revered by our peoples for his knowledge of the heavens above has divined a pattern for you." Unfolding the top of the garment, the Master holds it up. With the slender forefinger of His left hand, He points. "Here are you, my brother," He looks tenderly at the Holy One. "And here, and here, are those with you." The pattern is filled with the colors of the precious dyes brought to the Expectant Ones by the adepts in the School of the Prophets. "And here is your truth and the embrace of that which you call God." Folding the garment carefully, the Master delicately hands it to His Holiness.

The lama bends, placing his forehead upon the garment now resting between his two outstretched hands. Rocking ever so gently, he begins a beautiful melodic chant. Because his head and body are bent, an observer could not tell that the chant emanates from him, but would assume that it must come, indeed, from realms beyond.

As though some unseen signal were given, two of the priests to the lama's right and left begin to do the same. Eyes closed, their hands folded and raised, they rock, initiating their own chant, their voices embracing the lama's.

A young one has come to be seated and, kneeling to the Master's left, speaks softly. "His Holiness returns the prayers many-fold over unto the sweet hearts, and yours, which have given this gift so precious to Him and our people."

The workmanship is resplendent. The lama is seated across a rectangular structure that contains dazzling white sand. To his right and left are a goodly number of small earthenware urns in which remarkably beautiful colored sands are placed. At the opposite ends of the rectangle are many of the priests in service to him. On the side where the Master is seated on an intricately embroidered, tasseled cushion are the other Essenes and behind them, as ever, the guardians.

As the lama reaches out with his left hand, one of his aides places a small container in it. The lama, his eyes transfixed as though upon some unseen object in the midst of the rectangle's radiant white sand, reaches out to slowly pour a most delicate stream of beautiful rose-colored sand onto the white. His hand and arm move with stunning rapidity, as if being coordinated by some mechanical device and not by mere physical agency. As he reaches out to the side with his right hand, another aide gives him a second small urn.

In what seems to be only moments, the pattern embroidered upon the gift woven by the Holy Maidens, the pattern foretold and guided by Rebochien and borne on this journey in the sacred keeping of the great warrior priests, the guardians, is now mirrored perfectly upon the sand! The lama has not only committed it to his mind and heart, but, amazingly, has directed his physical body to be an instrument to replicate it in the sands of this sacred chamber.

The Master smiles as He looks upon the deft movement of the lama's hands.

Finishing his work, the lama looks up smiling, his hands

palms up in his lap, his legs folded beneath him. "We shall offer many prayers over this." He gestures to the symbol before him. "And we shall, as we do so, be with you in your journey."

Their eyes intertwine, as though dancing on the rivers of light emanating from the two, from the wellspring of God's Light, that flows deep within each of them.

The days that follow are filled with discourses, the lama sharing the heritage of his past journeys in the Earth and the Master recounting His own journeys through the various temples of flesh that have brought Him to this point.

Their exchanges are on all topics, everything that the Master has had awakened within Him. He reveals to the lama the beautiful truths taught to Him by the Holy Maidens, those who nurtured Him throughout His childhood and awakened these truths within Him. The lama smiles and nods as though absorbing each word into his very being.

Then he reciprocates. And the Master, too, smiles and nods.

There are ceremonies and demonstrations, as some might term them, but these are truly expressions of their faith, their teachings, that which they hold sacred. The Master, observing all this, understands.

And within Him stir the ancient fires of times past ... the memory of the works at the Spring of healing water; the walks around the city walls behind which those who had persecuted His peoples were fortified; the evaluation of forces intended to embrace one another, but which moved instead in opposition. All this flows through His memory, His consciousness.

On the morning of His departure, the Master and the lama embrace wholeheartedly and, standing arms intertwined, promise to come together again in another world.

Once the Essenes leave the Sea, their journey becomes

incomparable, for now the lands are foreign to them, and moving through them brings encounters equally foreign to their customs and peoples.

As always, there are those who have gone before. Now those who did so many years ago to prepare the way joyously welcome the arrival of the Master and those with Him.

The rhythmic stomping of the soldiers' feet breaks the silence. Quickly, James, Jessie, and Moira draw their outer garments around their faces, throwing the loose edge up over their shoulders, as is the custom.

The column marches, clanking and rattling, then comes to a halt. Several soldiers are of obviously higher station, based on the colored garments over their shoulders and the several tassel-like ornaments dangling from them.

A corporal steps forward from the group and salutes its officer, who speaks in a strong, authoritative voice. "The outcome?"

"We have them."

"Captives?"

"Yes, a goodly number. We have them encamped beyond the wall." He gestures off to his right.

"Are they well secured?"

"Yes, sir. Well secured. And others of the garrison have come to strengthen our number."

"Very well, come in. Give me a full report. I want to know where these heathen zealots are. I have heard there is another group even further north. Come in!"

Jessie gasps and moans. Moira begins to rock.

James quickly reaches a hand across to stop her, "Do not! They will see you, and come over to question us. Look at them! They are like wild beasts ready to pounce on their prey, any prey, and that includes us."

Given this and the recent events, later as they walk back through the city streets, James has almost forgotten, but not

Moira. Her eyes dance now as she sees the place where the one who asked had been sprawled, his crippled form leaning against the wall. She reaches over to squeeze James' arm.

Jessie, on his other side, leans over, looking inquisitively at her.

James breaks into a smile and nods. "We have much before us to do. But we can take a bit of time. Let us check. I believe this is the place they would have chosen."

Moira knocks on the door.

The young lad opens the door. He looks fresh and bright, obviously taking good care of himself with the coin he was given to treat the one who was dis-eased.

"You look well." Moira smiles, tilting her head.

"I am." He bows and gestures his thanks. "Much to your generosity."

They look about the small, largely barren chamber in the lodging's entryway.

The lad laughs quietly. "Perhaps you would rather wait outside. The air is a bit better there. It is stuffy in here. I will join you in a few moments."

They glance at one another, and Jessie leads the way out of the portal where they find a place to sit against the lodging's outer wall.

Leaning back, James reflects on recent events, vividly imagining the terror that must have swept through their distant family. He cannot help but hope that some have survived. Some must carry on for the group. It must be so.

"Here he is!" The young lad grins, his arms supporting the dis-eased man who, though still laboring somewhat, moves with surprising agility.

"Oh, my good saviors, look you upon my body! What magic potion have you given me? Oh, it matters not. I thank you. How might I serve *you* now? I am not yet very strong, but look." He turns his hands over and over. "My fingers, they move again! And the swelling is nearly gone."

James smiles up at the figure standing before him. "Do you wish to serve that which has brought you healing?"

"Oh, yes! How can I ever repay? What do I, who have nothing, have to give to you?"

James stands. The dis-eased one looks up into James' eyes, for his stature is greater than his own. "This is what you have to give." James thrusts his forefinger against the man's chest. "Give from your heart. Just as we have given to you, know that God has given to you. And as you would, give unto others in turn, as we have given. Then it shall be given to you manyfold over for each good blessing you impart to another."

The dis-eased one twists his head this way and that. "Those are strange words. I have heard them before several times by that one from the wilderness." He turns to gesture. "He came and stood right over there, climbed up onto the wall of the well, and stood there. Not one solider accosted him." The man looks down and cackles loudly to himself. "Oh, I tell you. They will not lay a hand on that one. And those who are with him, they do just as … Wait! Are you with him? Are you one of those who tends such as I? Who casts out demons?"

"We are with that One God, whose work flows through each of us. To this extent, yes, he is our brother."

Suffer not unto yourselves, ever, the pangs of loneliness or fear. Believe not that that which has been of goodness and gladness to thy heart, mind, and spirit can ever be lost. For always in those times of questing, of calling out unto God, of seeking that which you believe to be lost, One stands at your side. He is our Brother.

Chapter Nine

Safe

The pathway inclines somewhat severely at this point of the journey to the sea. As they move noisily, laboriously, one soldier comments to the other, "I don't know why we need to take them all this distance to the sea."

"More money," he replies offhandedly. "And they want them out of these lands."

"Why? Most of them are just women. What harm can they do?"

"They can give birth to more Zealots," the second soldier growls. "Were it my decision, I would simply rid our lands of them once and for all."

"Well, like you said," the first responds, "money. Probably ten times what they would bring at market back there." He points his thumb over his shoulder.

The captives strive to keep their spirits bright. Glancing over their entourage, each of the maidens strives to tend to another who looks weary or appears to be in need. They are flanked by guards, soldiers walking some distance away who, stumbling over the strewn terrain, grumble and glance hostilely at those they are intended to guard.

The smell of food cooking begins to stimulate the noses of several soldiers. They look at one another with curiosity.

Astride his mount, their leader raises a hand to signal

alertness to the company and turns to look at his lieutenant. "Be on guard. Send several forward and see who is ahead. I do not like this." He looks up to the left and right. "Not much room to maneuver here. It could be a trap. Surely they must know we are taking some of their people to market."

"How could they know?" the lieutenant counters. "None know of this journey save those of our own garrison."

"Those Zealots," the captain responds briskly, "have eyes and ears everywhere. Now, do it!"

The lieutenant wheels, signaling to two others who are mounted, and they move briskly up the slope and over the top of the summit.

Mingled with the aroma of wondrous cooking now comes the sound of a stringed instrument and several voices in song and laughter.

After a time the lieutenant returns with his two cohorts and, coming to a wheeling turn in front of the column, falls in astride the captain.

"Well? What is it?"

"As you might expect on this path, sir … traders heavily laden with goods, probably just coming from the seaport."

"What is the look of them?"

"A mixture. The one I spoke to, definitely an easterner. Skin, eyes, clothing, everything, leaves no question, sir. These are merely a caravan of traders from the East, perhaps coming by sea. Who knows? But I can tell you this, there are some beauties there." He laughs aloud.

"And there they shall remain," the captain grumbles. "Very well, but send those two ahead and keep watch. Have them look to the outer sides."

"It is much more level there," the lieutenant reports, "over the rise."

"I know this path," the captain growls back. "It is not that level. It could yet be a trap. I would not put anything past them. Clever, vile lot."

Slowly, the captain and his men ease their mounts up to the edge of the encampment. Members of the caravan are gathered in small, scattered groups, drinking long drafts from skins they lift and spurt into their open mouths, laughing. There is food cooking over bold fires here and there. Over to the side, one strums a curious instrument, producing quite a pleasant sound, though its appearance would belie it.

Some maidens turn spits of roasting meats in large cookpots, seasoned with herbs and spices. The fragrances are delectable. A number of staved barrels line the upside of the left wall of boulders, and beasts of burden rest off to the far left and down a bit. Everything seems typical of a band of traders, barterers, and who knows what else.

Gazing off to the horizon at the rapidly dimming light, the lieutenant turns to the captain. "Why not camp here for the night, sir? They invited us to partake of their food with them. And look you, they have much."

"Too much! I cannot help but think that they anticipated us. Be on guard. Send several up to the ridges.' The captain points about, "There, there, over here, and there. I want a report. Tell them to be on watch for others, perhaps hidden."

"Very well, sir."

Soon the guards are atop the high positions indicated by the captain.

A report is returned shortly from a small group that has scouted the surrounding lands. "Nothing to be seen, sir."

"Maintain vigil!" Having dismounted, the captain straightens himself and then swaggers towards the campfire, followed to the right and left by his personal guards. "Who is in charge of this company?" he demands loudly.

"Well ..." One figure, seated on a rock and poking some meat turning on a spit before him, looks up casually. "I guess that would be me, sir."

"How are you called?"

"I'm called Iliam."

"And your home land?"

"Oh, far away, and not where I am coming from."

The captain points with a rod. "What do you have in those packets?"

"These are fine fabrics from the East. If you would be interested, I can make you a good offer. They say they are made from the droppings of little worms." Iliam throws his head back, laughing heartily.

Several of the others have brought loaves of bread and are breaking them and offering them along with skins of drink to some of the captain's company.

The captain stops them. "Hold that! We have our own."

"As you wish, Honorable One."

"Watch your tongue! It can come out as easily as that." His hand slices the air, as though it holds a sword.

"No offense, sir. Perhaps I have had a bit too much of this fine wine." With that, he lifts a flask to squirt another draught into his open mouth.

The lieutenant unconsciously rubs his stomach and works his lips as he watches members of the caravan come one by one and take foodstuffs from the large baskets, scooping ladles of enticing porridge and other fare from great urns, maidens moving in and out passing bowls of exotic fruits, dried, but quite fragrant.

Studying those noisily devouring the food, the captain finally growls. "Very well, but, mind you, I will be keeping a watchful eye." He seats himself on a robe laid down for him by one of his aides.

"Here, sir. Try this." He is handed a bowl filled with sumptuous meats, the fragrances of which would whet the appetite even of one who had just eaten a full meal, for the aromas of eastern herbs are unknown in these lands.

Poking around in the bowl, the captain preaches down and takes a small morsel. There is a pause and then his face brightens for the first time. "Outstanding! How have you seasoned these?"

"Oh, we have those herbs for purchase, as well, Your Highness." Iliam smiles. "I could make you a very good deal on them, sir."

"I have no time for such barter," the captain responds, more softly this time. "But I must say, these are delectable."

The maidens and some of the others, younger, so it would appear, make their way through the caravan of soldiers, handing out bundles of breads and vegetables that obviously have been carefully prepared. Two of the maidens bear enormous skins, one over each shoulder.

The captain raises his hand abruptly. "Hold!" He turns to the lieutenant, who has now seated himself nearby. "You! Go see to it that they take only that which is appropriate. I shall not have any falling drunk on my watch."

Rising, the lieutenant follows the maidens, joking with them, and they laugh. The maidens, whose faces are covered, still cannot hide the beauty of their being that shines from their eyes, which they use very adeptly. The lieutenant is nearly mesmerized, enchanted by the soft voices and the warm, round, dancing eyes.

As one bends to fill the bowl of a soldier resting on a rock near several of the captives, she steals a glance at them. They are studying her. Imperceptibly to the soldier she blinks to the captives and twitches her head back and forth.

Suddenly, one of them realizes that she is signaling and leans to whisper to one of the others. "Be on guard. I believe our peoples are in those garbs." The message passes stealthily, as the Expectant Ones strive to contain their excitement and joy.

The maiden straightens. "What of the captives, sir?"

"Nothing. Give them nothing."

"They might bring a better price if they are well fed. Do you not think it so?"

The lieutenant glances around looking at them. Most are

slouched over, their heads covered. "Let their God feed them."

From a distant slope he watches, carefully studying the angle of the sun's light. Turning, Nathanael reports quietly, "They have guards on the outer periphery."

James nods. "But not so many."

"Not so many at all," Nicodemus echoes. The rush of realizing what lies before them has inspired him. He would have the entire lot. Not one would be lost.

Jessie looks into his eyes. "Nicodemus, you should not be here."

"That may be, but there are those among that company of captives that I hold in my heart. My heart beats because of them."

"So is it for all of us," James responds quietly. "Still, it is true. I would feel better if you were not here. There are roving patrols. We saw several on our journey here from the Sacred Spring. We cannot chance your discovery. You are needed in the times ahead, for you can speak in our voice where we cannot, and of our spirit where it is needed."

Nicodemus sits up and looks about, then turns to two who are his students and nods. They all rise, embrace each of the others, and turn to walk back towards the city.

Jessie watches them slowly disappear into the fading light. "Imagine what he risked to be here, James. I so admire him. To live in their world and learn their ways, their law... What an effort that must have taken, and does take."

"Indeed." A pang of admiration rushes through his body.

He sits cross-legged, well beyond the sight of the guards on the northern periphery, staff lying across his lap as casually as if he stopped simply to admire the beauty of a sunset. "Is it well to be so exposed?"

Turning around to look into the eyes of Nathanael, John

answers the guardian lightly, "We are seen only when we want to be seen, are we not?" and laughs softly. "No, seriously, they cannot see us here."

Nathanael responds playfully, "If they cannot see us, how is it, then, that we see them?"

"Our sight is clearer," John whispers.

"The herbs we have placed in the wine should be affecting them soon," she whispers. "Indeed, look over there. Those two are struggling to keep their eyes open. Let us go sing and dance so no one will pay attention to them."

"That is a very good idea."

The two sisters move off arm in arm.

"Captain, you are headed to the sea, I gather?"

The captain yawns. "Yes, to the sea."

"It has become very busy there these days. Many more vessels coming and going from diverse places," Iliam mentions casually.

Leaning back against his ornate, outstretched robe, the captain yawns again.

"I have noticed that many Greeks are sculpting good works. We have some, if you would like to see them."

The captain stretches and leans back a bit further.

"And those in the lands of ..."

No more is heard. The captain's eyes flicker closed, as he draws in a deep breath and leans back to rest his head.

Continuing to drone on about whatever comes to mind, Iliam watches carefully. Soon the captain's breathing becomes deep and rhythmic and so does another's over there, and there. Soon all who can be seen are fast asleep.

A maiden moves with grace and ease up to the top of one of the summits.

The soldier posted there turns brusquely.

"I come to bring you food and drink."

He studies her carefully. "On whose order?"

"Why, your captain's. He said to remain where you are, but he does not want you enhungered or with thirst."

"What have you there?"

The maiden hands the soldier, who has relaxed a bit, a bowl, a linen with fresh bread, and a small flask. "As you can see, the same foods as we have, we offer to you. It is our custom to share. We believe that by sharing that which we have, greater comes to us."

The soldier sneers. "Sounds like some strange eastern teaching."

"Ah, yes. So it is. In our homeland we all live by these words."

Without speaking further, he seats himself on a nearby rock and begins to eat.

The maiden moves off a bit and studies him, watching, waiting, as he takes his first draft from the small wineskin.

"Now that is good wine!" He wipes his hand across his mouth.

"We have nothing but good wine and good merchandise, as well. If you should like to see them, I should be joyful to show them to you."

Even more relaxed now, the soldier smiles. "Well, perhaps so. It is too quiet up here. There is nothing out there." He gestures into the vastness lying beyond the slope. "They are afraid of shadows. Who would fear a bunch of rabble? Zealots or not, their spirit alone cannot match our skill, our weaponry. We are the best."

"Well, then, let me fetch some of our merchandise. Perhaps I could make a small gift of some to you. Do you like the herbs in that loaf?"

Looking down, the soldier takes a large mouthful in a single bite, chewing aggressively as he does, and nods. "Very strange, but what a wonderful taste!"

The maiden smiles, knowing that cooked within the loaf are herbs that she and her people know bring on a deep, sweet sleep. "Then I shall fetch you some in a pouch. You can take them with you and command those who cook for you to include them in your foods."

"Good, good, go and get them."

"Not all of them asleep," Nathanael whispers.

"Well then, we have some work before us," John whispers in return.

"You mean …?"

John shrugs his shoulders lightly. "Not a permanent sleep, a temporary one."

The movement from both sides is swift. James and the group with him and Nathanael, under the watchful eye of John, advance. Soon they are moving among the captives. The tearful cries of joy are met with hushed guarded responses, accompanied by sweet embraces.

"Come, all of you," Jessie whispers. "We must depart. Naught is to be left to chance. We have no true knowledge of what they are like, or how deeply they sleep."

Several guardians are standing watch over the array of deeply sleeping soldiers.

As the Expectant Ones move swiftly into the newness of the night, one asks, "Unto where do we journey?"

"To the Sacred Spring. No one, not even those," pointing back over her shoulder, "can harm us there."

Many songs are being sung, and many wounds are being tended. The elder Holy Maidens move about easily, joyfully, among these sisters who have come from their distant family.

"We have heard so much, Rachel," Anna begins compassionately, "and we understand that the children were sent to the south, to the lands of the Egyptians."

"Yes. And we thank God that we were able to dispatch them while the soldiers were being held at bay."

Judy nods, her eyes opening and closing as though she were departing, coming and going.

"What see you, my sister?" Anna asks.

"Naught of danger, naught of fear. Hardship, weariness, yes, but I think they are well. We could send some of our brethren to get news," she continues slowly, deliberately. "But I do not think it well to do that just yet. We should wait a while and let things settle. The Romans are in quite a stir, and we understand that some are being severely punished."

A little laughter comes from some of the maidens who had been captives.

"We understand your response," Judy acknowledges them softly. "But one needs to have compassion for the enemy as well as for friends. Most of them were simply doing what they were told, and doing what was necessary in order to survive. That was all they knew to do."

James is arranging embers under the cook-pot as John and many of the others converse guardedly so as not to be heard beyond the walls of this abode. "It is difficult to know whether or not any of them were recognized, but I think not."

"Well, that captain … He is furious and I understand he is to be punished severely by those in authority."

Shrugging her shoulders, Hannah responds softly, "It is not we who have wrought this upon him, Rebekah, but that which is the harvest of his earlier works."

Rebekah nods, as her eyes fill with tears over the memory of all her brothers and sisters who crossed over into the embrace of God, perhaps at the hands of these very soldiers.

The bright sun glistens upon the ornamented temples of these peoples. As He walks along, a small group surrounding Him, the Master looks this way and that, taking in the aromatic fragrance of incense and listening to the chanting. Along the pathway various merchants displaying fine fabrics bring to mind some of those worn by the adepts in the School of the Prophets.

"This way," the guide tells the Master.

They turn and follow him up a gentle slope and come before a beautiful ornate structure of bright, vibrant colors. Towards its center is a large bell-shaped object and several in fine garments who sparkle with the brilliance of their cleanliness, their heads glistening in the reflected light of the highly polished floors.

The Master leaves the small entourage and moves with ease and grace to stand before the ornate metallic object.

One steps to the forefront, a superbly embroidered garment about his shoulders and down towards the front. Its golden threads and fibers trace a remarkably delicate pattern embroidered all across the underlying fabric. His hands come together, and he bows.

The Master reciprocates, and they move over to the side where, in careful geometric pattern, a number of ornate cushions have been placed upon an equally ornate floor, its design created by inlaid patterns of astonishing colored woods.

Many topics of conversation ensue, along with smiles and nods from the entire company of this priest and his disciples.

Slowly he reaches into the folds of his outer garment and the golden sash about his mid-section and pulls forth a bit of white rolled up parchment. It is tied at the center with a shiny red fabric that hangs down in generous loops, obviously signets of a gift of honor or authority. In a ceremonial gesture or salute, he places this parchment-like fiber in his right hand, outstretched towards the Master, bends his left arm to place that hand on the forearm of his right, and then leans to lay his forehead upon his left forearm.

The Master is seated uprightly. He closes His eyes for a brief moment, which all present note. Reopening them, He extends His left hand to accept the small scroll. Simultaneously, with His right, He reaches out to take the high priest's bent left elbow in the palm of His hand and bending forward, leans to touch the top of His head to the top of the high priest's. "May your ancestors find eternal peace and joy in the embrace of the All," the Master begins quietly, His face pointed down at the ornate floor, "and may you and all those with you bear the eternal grace and blessings of the One God."

The great metallic object is struck vigorously. Throughout the open temple a mighty tone spills forth as though it were a waterfall cascading from the great ornate object.

All those below immediately fall to their knees. Near and far, the cone-like peaks that thrust themselves upward from the bosom of the earth are dotted with other priests who begin an ornate series of beautiful chants in answer to the temple toll. As one starts to fade, another resoundingly resumes the previous tones and adds another, until the lands all around are filled with the joyous sound of the prayers of this land's priests.

The gardens are resplendent. Wondrous hanging bushes overflow with fragrant flowers of all imaginable colors. Little pools of water harbor gaily-colored fish that do not swim away as the priests and the Master stroll by but seemingly with anticipation swim quickly to collect at the edge closest to where they walk, as though to greet them.

Slender reeds arranged in geometric patterns have within their spacious midst gaily-colored birds singing brightly, fluttering this way and that. The priest heads directly towards this. They pause in front of a door made of the same reeds. In its latch is a brightly sculpted pin.

The priest turns just a pace or two away from the Master and those with Him and, hands clasped, he bows again and again, speaking slowly in a sort of singsong tone.

The Master stands, His eyes closed, His hands together before Him.

Finally, with an expansive smile, the priest says to the Master joyfully, "As I open this portal and free these beautiful creations of our One God, O Brother, know that my prayer goes with them on their wings of beautiful color and light, and that their freedom to soar and sing to any who would see or hear them is my eternal prayer for you."

He turns and lifts the pin from the latch and opens awide the great door.

At first the beautiful creatures within only look curiously about, as though they would as well stay here with these beautiful people, as move out into what is thought of as freedom.

The Master smiles as He looks at them. "Ah, my brother, one is only imprisoned if they believe it so. But the spirit of those who tend these beautiful creations of our God is such that they know they are not imprisoned, but preserved within this chamber. And they know the love and peace in your heart, all of you." He gestures to the others who now ring this ceremony. "They seek not that which is perceived as freedom, for they know, do they not, that their freedom comes from within. Thou art," He spreads His hands wide, "the instrument of God giving unto the needs of these creatures. I thank you for the great honors you have given to me and to my brethren during our visit. I shall take the Truths you have imparted to me back to our homeland ... to be written, to be included in the great works that will be preserved in the hearts and minds of those who can truly be called our brothers and sisters.

"And I say unto you, my brother," He looks at the high priest, "the gifts of truth, the sacred teachings of your peoples, will long endure. For those who shall hold them, who shall be the repository of them, are as great guardians of light, the pillars upon which the truth of God rests."

The high priest bows.

Without another word, the Master moves slowly in long but graceful strides to walk into this large chamber. Immediately, many of the beautiful winged creatures come to alight on His shoulders and outstretched arms, singing gaily as they do. He turns about so the high priest and those with him can laugh. They clap their hands together, their heads bobbing, smiling, praising God for sending this One to their midst.

"We should get off the streets, do you not think it so?" Thaddeus whispers to Judas.

"Yes, but not until we reach them."

"It is a ways yet."

"Better to risk it than to miss anything they could share."

"Very well."

Preoccupied with studying the shadowy doorways that the group has been passing by, Thomas finally turns to Judas. "Several fine places of lodging are nearby. Perhaps it would be best if we take one of them and finish the journey on the morrow."

"No," Judas urges. "Please, I must see them. My heart will not beat another night without seeing them."

Thaddeus laughs quietly. "Well, we cannot have your heart stop. But let us hurry."

They move as silently as possible, on and on.

At last, Thomas knocks soundly on the door of an abode.

A small opening appears in the top of the portal, and Thomas sees an eye peering out at them. The dim remaining light glistens upon that eye as it studies those who seek entry. "How are you called and why do you come?"

Thaddeus makes the gesture of the Essenes, and the eye blinks several times. "Who is with you?"

Thaddeus speaks their names. "It is I, Thaddeus, and our brothers Judas and Thomas. We wish to see Nicodemus."

The opening closes.

There is silence for a period of time that becomes uncomfortable to Judas who fidgets as he looks this way and that.

Thomas smiles and whispers, "Even in this household there is a certain protocol, a certain rule, and he is merely following it. Abide in patience, brother."

At this, the door swings wide in one swift motion, making odd sounds as the levers grind against one another. A servant stands with his back and the door against the wall as Nicodemus raises his arms and laughs aloud. "Enter, enter my abode! Welcome! God be with you!"

Each of them salutes the abode and God's presence within it as they pass by the portal, touching the sacred symbols as they do. The door closes with a thud, and a large mantle is placed in its brackets to secure it.

Judas looks all about, his eyes dancing. "Where are the others?"

"In the courtyard," Nicodemus gestures. "But come you! Let me take your outer garments." He waves to one of his servants, who is actually more like family.

Having handed over their outer garments, they move into the courtyard, generous, rectangular in shape. Upon its posts sit small lamps, warming the area. Many Essenes are seated here and there, all of whom stand, offering greetings and gesturing to their hearts. The three newcomers then move all throughout the group greeting them in return.

Finally, with some excitement and an air of wonder and awe, they seat themselves at the appointed table, a goodly number of the Expectant Ones already having gathered.

"I heard the good news," Judas begins excitedly. "You

have rescued some of our brethren. Tell me of it."

James straightens himself in his typical manner. Studying Judas carefully, he glances to his right and left, and then back at him. "We have the sisters," he begins slowly, deliberately, "the Holy Maidens, and a few others, praise God." He strikes his chest. "We know of none that He will call who are unaccounted for. Some are still on their way here. But they are safe, we are told."

"Are many lost?" Judas' face indicates the pain he feels already.

Looking down, James responds reluctantly. "Yes, a great many. The children are already in the Egyptian lands, so we have been told by messengers of Elob."

"Praise them, Father! Praise them! Will they return soon?"

"I fear not."

"And you say all of the maidens whom we know He will call are safe?" Thaddeus asks.

Yes, safe."

A heaviness lingers, then from the front chamber, laughter can be heard, along with the sound of the great door opening and closing with its customary thud. Everyone pauses to see what the commotion is. A bit of apprehension begins to mingle with the anticipation, for with the recent aggression one can never tell when a similar confrontation might yet befall them.

A figure strides smoothly into the courtyard, stops at the portico and flings his arms high. "Ah, little brothers and sisters, I greet you."

Some laugh, some jump to their feet, many run to greet this voice from the wilderness. Turning to remove a rather burley outer garment, he hands it to a beautiful, young maiden who comes shyly. Her face flushes as John rests a palm against her cheek and tells her of her beauty. Then he speaks a little more loudly. "Guard my garment well. Much labor has gone into it, you know," and throws his head back laughing. "Many would say wasted labor." And he laughs again, striding over to boldly embrace all of his brothers and sisters, one by one.

Sitting across from Judas, where they have made a place for him, John leans ever so casually to put his elbow on the table and cup his chin in his hand. His eyes come to rest upon Judas so firmly that he begins to fidget about. The sight makes John smile. "Well, brother, how fare you in this life?"

Judas, glancing about, is a bit unnerved at first. Then, as John's other hand comes across the table to grasp his in an obvious gesture of love, he relaxes, his face softens, his eyes round. "Oh, I am well. I have heard much of your works. You honor us, my brother."

"Ah. The one who honors us is afar. All of us are but servants unto His word. But then, there is joy to be had in such service, is there not?"

Jessie has come 'round to lay a hand on John's shoulder. She stands, looking down at him.

John turns to look up into her eyes. "Well, little sister, I have heard many good things about you."

Without speaking, she nods.

"And our new little sister … You know, the one who spoke up for us at the river and at the well? Where is she? I would look upon her."

Jessie smiles, somewhat surprised that he would know what she intended to ask, and speaks for the first time. "Oh, she is filled with light. She is unquestionably of our people … in spirit, at least."

"Well, then, bring her forth that we might look upon her." John looks around as James laughs softly. Thaddeus follows John's gaze, while Judas simply sits, inspired and somewhat in awe of all that is transpiring.

As Jessie moves back into the shadows, John turns back to Judas and remarks, "You have spent some time afar, I understand."

"Yes, I have, with those of the sixth tribe."

"Beautiful people," John answers admiringly, "beautiful! Are they well? Last I heard they had taken measures to avoid the soldiers."

"Oh, yes, I believe they are quite safe."

"Good, good." John looks down at the table.

From around the portico come Nicodemus, Jessie, and a beautiful young maiden bedecked in shiny, clean garments. She glances about hesitantly. Noting her, John rises swiftly to his feet and gestures.

Laughing, Nicodemus prods her just a bit. Then Judas and Thaddeus shift a little, and James and his brother, John, move to make a place for her at the head of their table.

"Please, little sister, seat yourself. God's peace be with you ever," John begins softly. "From whence come you?"

"I come from Sodom."

John nods. "Ah, yes, to the north beyond Tyre."

"Yes," she answers quietly.

"And your family, your parents?"

"Gone," she answers, with almost no emotion. Obviously many years have passed to soften the pain of her wounded heart.

John, sensing this, reaches out his hand.

She hesitates for a moment, glancing up at Jessie and Moira, who have now come around. They nod affirmatively, and she turns quickly back, her beautiful rounded eyes gazing at John in wonder as she places her hand in his.

"My Brother will be pleased to look upon you upon His return. For I see in you, sweet sister, the song of the Promise. I know that you will walk with Him, and perhaps you will nurture Him unto His needs."

She looks down, her eyes fluttering, uneasy with the honor that is being placed upon her.

"I think it appropriate, and I know my Brother speaks it

to me in these words, that on behalf of Him and our peoples, thou art welcomed as sister."

Many utter little sounds of affirmation, little prayers, welcomes. Some strike their chests, others look up. Some are bobbing their heads in a silent prayer of blessing to this, their new sister.

"But, then, it is appropriate among our peoples that you should be named in our family. What say you, brothers and sisters?"

All speak animatedly and raise a hand to affirm this.

After a brief time, John, gazing at all of them, turns with a sweet gentleness in his eye. "What would He say of thee? Let me see ..." John rubs his chin with one hand, his eyes glisten with the merriment of what he is about. "Thou art truly a flower of God. And my brother, my sweet brother, Iliam, has told me of one such flower, and so I would give its name to you. Thou art the sweetness of jasmine. Let it be so. What say you, brothers and sisters?"

Silence. John looks about, his face somewhat blank, expressionless. Then he tilts his head back and begins to laugh very gently. "Well, so much for that." He turns back to look at the young maiden. "You would honor the name, as the name has been honored, if you could be called Miriam, after an elder Sister whom I have known of that same name."

Many voices speak in wonder and awe. For they know of the one whom the Master has called by that name as well as another.

She looks down and covers her face with her free hand, weeping tears of joy.

$$\LARGE \text{✦}$$

In the peacefulness of that which is borne

*on the spirit of God's living Light, many beau-
tiful things can be found. So is it within nature
that the voice of God speaks silently unto the
Earth and calls it forth to bear all manner of
good things unto the Children of God. And so
is it, then, that each can call within themselves
in the same manner, a brilliant, beautiful
bounty of harvest.*

*For as the Spirit of God is in the Earth in
that which you call nature, so must it also be
within you. And as the good seeds sown into
the warm earth can be nurtured and bring
forth good bloom, good fruit, so must it be for
each of you.*

*Thus we leave you here with that as our
prayer, that you would ever know the beautiful
bloom of that which lies within, and that you
bear a good harvest from same and offer it unto all who come before you. In that same spirit
of this prayer for you, so do we offer unto you
that which we have as our harvest.*

Chapter Ten

𝕲ifts of the 𝕾eed

arge blankets are spread out upon the slope leading down to the Great Sea. Many leaves and berries, as well as roots rest there, set out to dry in the warmth of the mid-day sun.

Eloise is guiding several of the younger maidens as to which herbs should be placed in containers with others, and which should not. She laughs aloud at the comment about all the different combinations and how does one remember them all. Smiling down at one of the younger maidens, she remembers those earlier times when she and the Holy Sisters also struggled to understand all the nuances and subtleties of the various herbs and their interactions with one another.

She looks across the way to see many of the Holy Sisters standing near the great cook-pot, stirring, adding bits of this or that, and generally relaxing with the new wards entrusted to them by their families, the tribes from the north.

"There is no need to squeeze those roots. The cooking will release the juices," Hannah explains tenderly to a little one barely tall enough to see over the top of the pot.

"But they smell so good when you squeeze them," she giggles.

Still stirring, Hannah reaches over to stroke the child's forehead, absentmindedly brushing her hair back as her mind wanders. She remembers a time when Judy stood by a pot just like this and spoke to her about all that can be perceived, inwardly and outwardly, if one but seeks and listens.

Her thoughts are interrupted as her sister Kelleth steps forward and bends over to inhale deeply the fragrances coming from the cook-pot. "Well, I look forward to this meal." She turns to smile at Hannah.

Nodding, Hannah watches the little girl scamper off to play with a number of her brethren. "Have you heard any news about Mary?" Hannah asks softly as she peers into the bubbling broth.

"Yes, many activities are ongoing, teaching those who were with the other tribes. And there is a lot of interaction between the followers of John and those being prepared for His return."

Hannah looks up to make eye contact with her Sister. "Has anyone heard … you know, about when that might be?"

Now Kelleth studies the boiling broth, her face becoming wistful. "A number of years yet, I suspect, though we await a message from the East."

"They are all free," the merchant reports quietly. He is sitting in a small valley just above the river.

John, leaning back, runs his hand across the spring flowers that are blooming profusely here. Turning to look at the merchant, he smiles. "Do you feel free?"

The merchant rubs both sides of his face simultaneously. "I tell you, John, I feel more than free. What I feel is a sense of purpose in life. I want to share with you that I not only have I seen to it that all those for whose bondage I was responsible are now free, but I also liquidated everything and gave each one some compensation for what I had done."

"How did they receive your gifts and their freedom?"

The merchant laughs as he recalls that almost all of them were in disbelief. "Then when I gave them coin, my penance of sorts, many of them simply stood staring down at it and then up at me. And as my means permitted, I also procured the freedom of a number of others, whom I knew not."

"How were you guided to do this?" John asks, studying the merchant's face.

"It was curious. I felt as though something was pulling at me right here." He taps his fingertips upon his solar plexus. "It got warm, almost hot sometimes. So I closed my eyes and remembered your words. That is how I knew."

"That is a good way of knowing, Merchant. In fact, one of the best." John smiles happily.

To John's right are seated a goodly number of those who are often, if not constantly, with him and many gathered here who had been raised by the Essenes and then sent into the outlands. These are those John has found and reawakened unto the Word and the teaching. So a sizable number is arrayed here, the sun shining warmly on them. Even the flowers lift their faces, as though to receive, according to the word of John, a special blessing from God.

"What will you do now?" asks little Miriam, who is only several paces away from John.

The merchant turns to smile at her. "As you, I suspect, little sister, if I might call you that."

Many laugh, for clearly the merchant is welcomed here, and there are no barriers, no limitations. All are seen as equals.

Little Miriam moves closer, perhaps an arm's length from the merchant, and looks at him, her eyes softening. She turns back to John and to Justus, who has moved to sit beside him. "Would it not be wonderful, so wonderful, if all the world could do as the merchant has done?" She leans over to rest her hand on his shoulder. The merchant's face flushes, and he looks down and then back up at little Miriam. "Think about it. If we were all in harmony, if the world did not see the gifts and blessings of others as threats, but as true gifts, each day would be a sacred celebration."

Stretched out on the valley's upslope, still leaning on one elbow, John replies, "Perhaps it shall come to pass. Perhaps you are prophesying that which shall be, little sister."

She flushes and momentarily bows her head. Then she looks up and turns to the merchant. "I so admire you. "Only … How long has it been? Not a year, and here you are. I remember it so well, do you not?" She points down the slope to the river's edge and laughs softly. "Right over there is where you stood, defiant."

Justus quietly observes, "I saw it as pleading."

The merchant studies him. "You are the one He … He healed, are you not?"

"That I am," Justus acknowledges readily.

"Well …" The merchant ponders Justus' leg and extends his right hand and arm, remembering only too well that which had visited his own body. "I know whereof my transgressions came … forgive me for calling them such. But I consider them often. Might I ask, from whence came yours? As I have been told you were but a lad."

Resting his palms upon the earth behind him, Justus leans back and looks up at the beautiful clouds passing by. "Mine came from God," he answers quietly.

Silence.

The merchant shakes his head, uncomprehendingly.

"There is much to be shared and learned among us all," Nathanael adds for the others who have again moved closer to this group to share. "Many answers can be given to questions such as these."

John looks down at the flowers before him, again gently running his hand across their heads, and glances up to meet the eyes of his dear friend, Iliam, now fixed upon him, and smiles.

Iliam merely nods, returning the gaze and smile. "I think it would be good for our new brother to be renamed."

John, still smiling at Iliam, raises himself to a sitting position. Wiggling this way and that as though to indicate that something is coming, he brings his hands together and tips his head up slightly. In that very moment, a cloud passes over the sun's face and there is a period of shadow over the group, and specifically over John. He opens his eyes and glancing around, smiles. "Perhaps this is an indication from God to go within. Let us do so." Again, his eyes close.

"O Lord God, we give thanks unto Thee for the return of our brother, who is now before us. We ask of Thee, grant him Thy eternal peace. We ask further on his behalf that Thou wouldst ever guide him, that whatsoever he shall come upon that might seem as a challenge be opened unto him, that he can look within and find that it bears him a gift delivered by Thy hand. Speak unto me now, Lord God. Give us a name, that he shall be reborn, as his spirit has already done so."

A prolonged silence falls while all in the group follow John's lead.

Some are smiling deeply. Others are so still they appear to be asleep. Some seem aglow. Then, the cloud passes and the sun shines upon them once again.

"Thank You, Father. We all thank You for Your gifts and Your guidance." John opens his eyes to look at the merchant, who has done his best to follow suit with his new brothers and sisters, and so, too, is seated erectly. "Thou art to be called Jeremiah."

The merchant's face twitches, its muscles moving this way and that, and his eyes pop open. Though his mouth, too, is open, no words come forth for a moment or two. "Jeremiah! Thank you."

John, smiling, points his finger up towards the sky. "Thank God. He gave it. I only repeated it." He laughs softly, rising to his feet to walk over and extend his hands.

Jeremiah stands to embrace him. Then all come to embrace Jeremiah and welcome him into their family of one.

"There is no way to know from just looking." Abigale turns the leaves over this way and that. "They must be felt to know whether or not they are ready." She rubs her thumb and forefinger over the leaves. "And when you break them," snapping one of the leaves in half, "you should then be able to smell and immediately know that they are ready, that they are dry enough."

One of the children in the small group to whom she is speaking raises his hand. "Abigale, when they are dried and stored in the urns we have prepared, how long will they be safe for us to use?"

"Ah-h." She smiles, reaching to joggle a leaf here, and a root there. "If we have taken care that the glazing on the urns is sufficient, and we seal them, then, indeed, they are usable for a great long time.

"These others, though," she gathers up a handful of berries, "and these over here," grabbing a handful of roots, "do not endure quite as long. They can be used for several years, but their vibrancy, their potency, begins to diminish after that."

Another little hand pops up. "Why do we grind some and make them into powders, and others we do not?"

Releasing the handfuls of berries and roots that she had gathered up, Abigale brushes her hands together. "Those which we grind into small bits, or into powders, are usually those that we put into the pouches and give unto our peoples. Those are the ones that have more medicinal and healing properties. By placing them into these fragmented forms, they will remain consistent. For when one of our brothers and sisters is out and about and needs to use some of these for healing works, it must always be that the same quantity will have the same effect, the same power within it."

The streets are particularly noisy this day. Many people are gathering for various springtime celebrations. As they move about the streets, carefully covering themselves to preserve their identity, Judas speaks quietly. "Well, James, though I do not like these crowds particularly, it would seem to me that they work to our advantage."

"Indeed."

"How many do you suppose there are?"

"From what I have heard, not very many ... perhaps ten, twelve."

"And these were gathered by the patrols?"

"Yes," James responds. "Apparently they had fled during the soldiers' attack."

Arriving at the square, the multitude is sizeable: merchants offering various wares, traders from distant places marketing and calling out this or that price for their goods. It is a curious collage of peoples. Some obviously are of stature and wealth, others have guards, servants in some cases, who are protecting them from the pushing and shoving.

"How will we go about bidding without calling attention to ourselves?" Judas asks.

"We shan't. Some time back, we made a friend. He was dis-eased." He turns to glance at Little Miriam, who smiles. "And now he is well. He has become somewhat adept at such matters, so he will do the bidding for us."

"Praise, God! All our teachings are of truth. We gave to him that which we had to give, our prayers and the herbs of our peoples, and he was made whole. And look at him, James ... He is now a bright light for us."

"And, I might add, very useful. He is accepted and can act without raising suspicion when the rest of us might be on delicate ground." James smiles, pointing over to the soldiers gathered by the gate.

The sound of the waves gently breaking against the bow of the boat has a hypnotic effect. Several of the Essenes who have been journeying with the Master are resting against the gunwales, an arm propped up on the side rail here, feet placed upon coils of rope there. It is a casual, easy day.

"It is truly awesome," begins the one seated closest to the Master. "The wisdom and knowledge that has been gathered, added to that which we have learned from you and all our good teachers, the Holy Maidens, the teachers at the good School ... wondrous! But I ask of you, Lord, what shall come of this? It is a treasure for the world, and yet, only we and a small number know of it. What can be done to preserve it?"

His elbow resting upon a small wooden flask to His left, the Master rubs His chin and the side of His face. "God will guide us. But know this, my sweet brother ... It will be preserved. There are those who are one with us, who are awaiting our return. They will take these truths, ours and theirs, and they will preserve them."

"That is good!" It brings joy to my heart and my spirit. For I know there will be a time when," the Essene gestures with a sweeping motion of his arm towards the horizon, "the world will be ready to receive these ancient teachings. And perhaps," he leans back again, "even ready to live them."

The Master, looking upon him with warm, loving eyes, merely nods.

"We are indeed joyful to have you here with us," Elob begins softly.

"It is an honor," Marta adds.

"We shall start," he continues, "by comparing our teaching and heritage with yours ..." Studying the stately countenance of the group before him, he adds, "of the One God."

"That is a good beginning," the head priest responds. "And we are joyful, as well, to be with all of you." He gestures to all of the adepts who are gathered with the great teachers and seers in the School of the Prophets.

He then points to the sides. Several aides come forth bearing cloth wrappings and gently lay them down. The priest leans over to open one, revealing a scroll that he spreads out before him carefully and with some reverence. Pointing, he speaks quietly to Elob. "These represent a portion of our studies of the truths we have collected from diverse places and from ancient teachers. These also include teachings from our homelands to the north that are unknown to you here. When the Promise returns, we will add unto these those teachings of our brothers and sisters to the East and beyond our borders, along with yours. And it shall be a legacy of truth ... those pillars upon which the Spirit of God's Light might one day be held and seen openly among all peoples."

"You must be able to secure the top of the pouch completely," Andra demonstrates to the children who are busy making herb pouches for their peoples.

"I can not get this to work as well as she does," Daniel points to a young sister, off to his left.

She simply smiles, saying nothing as her hands move, deftly creating yet another pouch, weaving the thongs and braided fabrics as laces into the top portion. Then, jerking them closed snugly with a pop, she smiles again, looking around to make certain that someone else has seen her work.

"It is not always what one does, Daniel, but what one intends," Andra offers quietly.

"Well, if what I intend does not come out to be a pouch secure enough to keep the herbs preserved, what good is it?"

Andra glances to her side at Zephorah who is struggling not to laugh, then turns back to Daniel. "The meaning greater than a pouch. Your intention is what goes before you in all that you do, all that you are. This is one of the truths that we are striving to give to you."

"What good are those truths?" Daniel tosses his unacceptable pouch off to the side.

In silence Andra and Zephorah look at the pouch lying on the ground.

Andra leans over, picks up the pouch and turns it about. "What do you see wrong with this?"

"It does not work."

On the verge of laughter herself, Andra persists. "And, why does it not work?"

"I do not know. Look at hers," pointing again to the shy little girl off to his side. "Hers always work, mine do not."

Zephorah is chuckling now, she cannot help it. Leaning over, she whispers into Andra's ear, "Does he remind you of anyone?"

Without answering, Andra bends over to hold the pouch in front of Daniel. "Look here. You missed all these holes. That is the only reason it does not work for you."

"Well, I cannot get it through them."

"In life, little Daniel, you will find situations where you do not think you can get through something, but if you step back from it, and study it, look at all its aspects, you will find that even in the worst of challenges, there is something special for you ... a gift."

Reaching out to take the dangling pouch from Andra's hand, Daniel looks at it, turning it about. "All right, then." Reaching to pick up a small awl that is used to make holes in the leather, he twists it this way and that into the ones he had missed. "Like that?"

"Like that." Andra smiles.

Off to the side, Zephorah is still chuckling as she busily helps several of the other children.

"So, let me understand," Daniel continues, weaving the thong through all of the holes this time. "When I get big and I am out in the outer world, like some of my elder brothers and sisters are right now," he strikes his chest in a momentary prayer for them, "if I persevere ... Is that not what you said? If I persevere and pick up this awl and make the holes bigger, I can do that in life, too?"

Andra nods and smiles most warmly. "You can do that in

life, too. Just make the holes bigger so you can pass through them."

Grasping a generous handful of the muddy soil at the river's edge, Andrew bends to smear it all over the calf and knee of the one who has come seeking aid. He glances about, noting that many of his brethren are busy as well, tending to the needs of those who come here almost daily now, seeking healing, or ointment, or balm.

Smiling, he reaches inside his outer coat and finding just the pouch of herbs he wants, grabs a great pinch and sprinkles it on the bare skin of the boy's leg, covering it, as well, with the clay. Reaching a hand out, he receives a long swatch of cloth from Miriam and begins to wrap it around the poultice he has just applied. "Well, that should do nicely." Andrew gestures to the boy's parents. "Have him keep his weight off of it. It will dry and get as hard as this." He taps on a small boulder off to the side. "Hard. But he could crack it, and if that happens, it will not be of much use. So do watch over him. Keep him inactive."

"How long shall we leave it in place?" the father asks.

Andrew looks up at the sky as though some instruction were written upon it. "Five, six days should do. Then bring him here, and we will remove it to be certain it is well."

The mother comes to kneel before Andrew, hands together, a tear flowing from one eye. "Thank you. We feared he might never walk."

"He will walk." Andrew assures her with a smile. He reaches up and places one palm against the lad's forehead and another up into the air. "Lord God, bless this, Thy son, unto the goodness of Thy Spirit within him. I ask this of You in the Name of our Brother, knowing that His Spirit and mine together open the way, and that he shall be healed."

Turning to cup the boy's face in his hands, Andrew looks closely at it, deep into his eyes. "The healing will come from within you as much as without. But if you are to remain whole and healthy and well, the healing must be nourished as your body must be nourished. That nourishment comes from here." He taps him on the heart. "Know that there is a God. Know that that God loves you. He has breathed life into you here. And just as," gesturing to his mother and father, "they give you life now, so might you from here," tapping him on the chest again, "give life to others in the future."

Struggling to his feet, the young lad takes a staff from his father and an arm from his mother. He looks down at Andrew, who is still kneeling, hands covered with the mud, still looking up at him. "I will do that," the lad promises, smiling. "I remember how I was before you and your peoples gave unto us." He glances about the many gathered here. "I will not forget that pain. And I will not forget you. I want to be just like you. Can I call you my brother?"

Andrew looks down very quickly, struggling to contain a surge of emotion, and then back up at him. "It shall be my honor if you would."

The small family turns to begin their long, slow journey back to the city.

The movement is slow, almost arduous, for the children are weary. Yet the guardians continue to guide them through the night.

"How much longer?" one of the children asks a guardian by his side.

"Only one more day and night," he whispers.

"What shall we do in the lands of the Egyptians?"

"We have many sweet brothers and sisters who dwell there. And it is not something we will do forever, but only until we are ready and strong, and the challenge is gone."

Glancing over his shoulder, remembering what he left behind, the guardian walks slowly, in measured, almost mechanical steps. His thoughts race over his fallen wards.

And he thinks of his brothers, the other guardians, who have been left behind. Turning his attention back, looking across the small group of children as they continue to move through the night, his heart receives a message from his brothers, as though to say, *We are always one. No matter where we are, we are always one.* He nods and smiles as he continues the journey.

"That is a relief." James sighs deeply as they move. He looks back at the city and the closed gates, and then smiles down at the children they have purchased at auction.

Moira and Jessie weave in and out, tending first to the ones who are weary and then to the needs of the whole group.

"Eleven." James tallies as though speaking to someone unseen. "I wonder if there are others."

They argue vociferously, shaking their official signets at one another, tasseled ornate rods serving as emblems of office.

"You cannot tell me that these people are not a threat! Those who are out there by the river ..." He gestures towards a wall. "Each day their number grows. They are converting our people with their gibberish. I tell you, this is serious."

One of the other priests leans back on an ornate cushion and straightens his equally ornate garb. "It is being tended to."

"Not well enough," another calls out. "I have seen them in the city ... in the city, itself! They think they are unseen, but there is something about them. One look into their eyes and you know. You see the defiance. They truly believe that a king is coming. No, they think he is here! Where, I not know. Then there is that prophet by the river's edge, and those who are equally troublesome who are with him. Have you not heard? They are going all about the lands just like him. People come to them in droves, seeking healing, seeking food, seeking who knows what."

Several on the outer tiers who hold various positions of council and authority, some who are advisors, some who have great knowledge of the law and ancient teachings, are talking among themselves.

One of the priests points to Nicodemus. "What do you know? You journey often to many of the other cities and villages."

Very casually, Nicodemus receives this half question, half challenge, sensing from this one a threat to the Promise. "I have heard nothing that is troublesome for us."

Many of the other priests frown and mutter.

One comments in a voice audible enough to be heard, "That depends on how you define *trouble*."

Only glancing at him, Nicodemus does not answer directly, but continues, "Actually, they are doing us a service, if you will hear me out."

"And what might that be?" the priest asks.

"Think about it. They seem to take on those who are the worst of our peoples. They take the orphans, the diseased, and while I know not what happens to them," he smiles, glancing at the angry priest off to his left, "they are no longer our concern, are they? I mean, if we do not have to care for them, if we do not have to pass by them every time we want to go to a certain place in the city, our lives are better."

"Are you sure they are not recruiting them?" the head priest counters.

"I think not. At least not … well, not like the Zealots do, if that is your meaning. They seem content to teach them, to heal them, even provide for them. How, I know not."

Nicodemus glances down, eyes flickering as he utters a quiet prayer for forgiveness for he knows his words to be untrue. He quickly looks up again. "It is easy to distinguish the Zealots from these people. If you look at them, they are not preaching conflict or hostility. Quite the contrary, like that prophet … His voice and manner are strong, bold, even brash. But if you listen to his words, as I know almost all of you have …" They look at one another, suddenly recognizing that every one of them has quietly moved amongst the crowds to hear that prophet speak.

"Well," Nicodemus resumes softly, "he may shout at people to do various things, like repent, or forgive, or be kind to one another, but, honored priests, this is not one we need fear. Indeed, we should welcome such urging to our peoples. Better to call them forth in such a manner than to have to quell uprisings with a sword." He raises his embroidered, tasseled signet of office to the priests gathered. "Thank you for hearing me," he adds, nodding several times.

"I suppose there is truth to this," one of the priests begins quietly. "But yet there is something about it that concerns me. If they are grooming someone, somewhere to come forward and to say that he is the king, what then?"

"Indeed, what then?" contends another of the priests. "I say, continue to encourage the Romans and their guard to gather as many as they can and disburse them."

"Well, either way," the first priest counters, "both ends are met, are they not? Who knows, perhaps these Romans in their bumbling efforts will actually find the one they are grooming and send him away."

There is a bit of laughter at the thought of this.

"I dreamt of Him. And you are right, my sweet wife … He has given me a gift."

Moistening his brow with a damp cloth, Mary looks into Joseph's eyes. "Thank you, God. For if among our peoples there is one who is worthy of such a gift from the Promise, from our son, it is you, my sweet husband."

As She continues to wipe Joseph's face by moistening the cloth from the basin nearby, he lifts a hand to grasp Hers. "I would tell you of the gift."

Laying the cloth down and assuming a position of reverence and respect, She looks lovingly into Joseph's eyes.

"As I was in prayer on the eve before last, I called out, yet I heard naught. But during sleep this past night, He came in answer to my call. We walked hand in hand by a beautiful stream. The waters within it glistened and shined. And as they moved across the rocks beneath the surface, it seemed the waters were singing, and lights flashed beautifully, softly, all about. And we came to a place like our Spring, my sweet wife." They pause to reflect upon the Sacred Spring for a moment.

"Then we stopped and turned. While He still held my hand, He pointed across the stream to the distant shore. And as we looked into one another's eyes, He said, *The greatest of all gifts awaits you across this river of life in the lands beyond. There, my Father has prepared a house for you.*

"And the sweetness, my dear wife, that poured from His eyes … I tell you, the world will rejoice when He returns, and they see it as I have. Now I feel only the anticipation of crossing that small river, and the excitement and joy of what lies beyond. The gift He gave to me was to open my eyes that I could see … that I, Joseph, could see the Promise!"

Wheresoever you would look, your eyes might perceive this or that. Your heart might feel some emotion. Your mind might begin to reason, as it has been trained to do.

But if you would call upon Him to open the sight of your spirit, then surely you, too, sweet brothers and sisters, surely you shall see the Promise of God.

Chapter Eleven

Dost Thou Call Me?

It was nearly twilight when the vessel docked, giving them the cover of darkness to disembark and unload the items they had gathered upon the Master's journeys. Having done so, they placed their cargo onto carts and made their way out of the seaport to its edge. There they found the caravan awaiting them and embraced those sent to meet Him: Justus, Jeremiah, Nathanael, James, Andrew, Sarah the younger, Eloise the younger, Miriam the younger, Andra, Abigale, Hannah, and Zephorah.

Unto these there were given great gifts of joy and the embrace of the Master. Yet, they did not tarry, but loaded their goods on the beasts of burden and, veiled by moonlight, began their journey south towards the City of knowledge, the Great Library.

Upon reaching the designated point, they paused, en-camping, and discussing much.

Arising in the morn, those from Jerusalem, the sacred mountains, the great School, and elsewhere (who had split into small groups so their movement would be inconspicuous) all come to greet the Master and the others, each carrying a portion of those precious gifts that He had assigned unto them as caretakers.

The caravan quietly resumes its journey south, somewhat inland but quite near the sea, the only sound the jingling of the ornaments ever dangling from the tasseled pads on the beasts of burden.

"Why do you think they placed those jingly things on the camels?" one inquires.

"They say," responds another, "it is to drive away evil spirits, but it seems to me it gives away our coming." He chuckles softly to himself.

"Well, out here it would be difficult not to be observed or heard."

As the caravan continues its journey, some move about its considerable length. In its midst, Nicodemus speaks with the Master as they walk along slowly. "What has been the measure of your journey, O Brother?"

"Much," the Master responds softly. "Much has been given and much has been received."

Nicodemus glances at several of the bundles so carefully wrapped and secured on the camels before them. "I cannot wait to learn of these."

The Master's smile is soft as He extends a hand to tap His forefinger upon Nicodemus' chest. "You already have them in the best place of all ... right here."

"Ah, but it is here that I would like to know of them." Not one to be taken off guard Nicodemus taps his own forehead.

The Master laughs heartily. "Knowing things here," He taps His own forehead, "is a wonderful thing, indeed. For thou art knowledgeable, my brother." He looks at Nicodemus. "But the issue is not so much what one has in one's mind, but what one has in heart, for it is the heart that speaks. It is the heart that holds life eternal, and it is the heart that can heal. The mind knows many things, but the heart gives them life."

Always one to hold the Master's words as a treasure, Nicodemus falls silent. Pondering them, he hurries to keep up with the Master's long, easy, strides.

"Did you see Him?"

"Oh, we did. He looks wonderful. He is a man now, and His skin has mellowed and is beautiful. His eyes … They have a greater light than ever, and He speaks with the ease of one holding great wisdom."

Anna and Judy sit with their eyes closed, rocking gently as they listen to the recounting of the Holy Maidens and other sisters home from greeting the Master, newly returned from His journeys.

Justus is pacing all about, waving his arms then folding them within his garment, muttering quietly to himself.

"What is the matter with you, Justus?" Andra asks quietly, but with a measure of authority.

"I cannot stand this."

"What?"

"I have just seen Him again after all these years, and now we are separated again. I want to go to the School and be with Him and the others. Why can we not do this?"

Andra looks over at Abigale, Zephorah, and Hannah, who are also clearly longing to be with the Lord. "Remember the Promise," she suggests, glancing over at Anna and Judy.

Then Little Sophie, who is seated beside Judy, reaches a hand out.

Judy takes it. "Speak, little sister."

"My heart is filled with the joyful wonder that it is so. He has fulfilled the prophecy; He has placed the Promise in diverse places and received the gifts of truth from those who are the messengers of God in each land. And to think that even as we speak, He walks upon our lands again! Oh, my heart leaps just to think of it." She turns to Justus. "Come. Sit by me, take my hand and I shall place into your heart the gladness and peace that are within mine."

Looking down at her, Justus smiles, for he knows that she can do this. He seats himself, and to his other side comes the younger Eloise, who takes his other hand. "Look at you, how grown you are. I remember when you first came unto us," Eloise chuckles. "And now, few of us can encounter you without having to look up to see into your eyes."

The ceremonial fires are very small and not built upon the ground, but in special urns. Yet the inside of the great meeting chamber at the School is well illuminated by them. Tending each of the sacred flames are two of the adepts, each one representing the balancing forces of that point of the geometric pattern made manifest by the careful placing of the flames.

At the upper point from the entranceway we see the priests seated, four of them, garbed in their ornamental ceremonial robes. Each one is wearing a special headdress with its own unique meaning and purpose; for in accordance with their ancient teachings, it is intended to awaken specific levels of awareness. After their prayer, which is barely audible, the four reach out to grasp one another's hands in a small quadrangle. Then, dutifully, one takes a position behind the north point, another to the south, and each of the others to the west and east of the geometric pattern.

All about them are many of the great teachers, prophets, and seers. Of course, Elob is the first to stand and speak. Stepping forward into the center of the geometric pattern, he extends his arms and turns about slowly to greet each one, pausing perhaps just a moment longer as his eyes connect with and embrace those of the Master.

"We are honored to have you all here," Elob begins, "and we thank you for your prayers, for your ceremonial gifts, and for the treasure which you bring in the form of your souls, your light. He gestures to the Master. "As we gather here to harvest the gathering of this, our Brother called Christ, may we join together in this prayer of oneness that the works we seek to preserve in the days ahead shall be those of the greatest possible light and hope for those who shall follow."

He brings his hands together, folding them first before his forehead, then his mouth, then his heart. With his arms bent at the elbow, palms up, he begins this low prayer.

"O Great One, see into our hearts and minds and give unto us that light of wisdom which is eternal. O Great One, awaken within each of us that which is eternal and guide us to bring it forth as an offering to all those who are gathered. O Great One, let us know of Thee as we commence these works in Thy Name and let the eternal Light of Thy Spirit be that which shines through each of us by intent and by offering. We hold in this moment the vision of each of our brothers and sisters wheresoever they may be in these moments, and we give them of our light."

There is a prolonged pause. Some in the group, which is circular in its layout, are swaying to the right and left. Some are seated erectly, heads bobbing slightly. Others are striking their chest with a clenched hand. Yet others are bent forward, almost touching the earth of the Great Hall.

So it is, all about, that each in their own way, according to their custom and their teaching, offers their spirit's light and all that is within them unto those who are loved and at a distance.

"I tell you, He is back," Andrew insists quietly.

Peter all but ignores his brother, pulling mightily on a great net over the bow of their small vessel. "And what does He say?" he finally asks over his shoulder.

"He speaks of the things He has seen and done and the works that they have completed, and they are incredible! I think we should go and find Him and be with Him."

His arms straining under the load of the net before him, Peter continues to pull, removing an occasional small fish and tossing it into a basket mid-ship. "I know not what you were taught about this," he turns to glance at his brother, "but we were told that He would come to us, not the other way around." With that, he turns to pull more of the net into the vessel.

"You are a stubborn one," Andrew protests, "but as is so oft the case, you are also correct. I can barely contain myself though, and I know we yet have a bit of a wait ... much too long for me."

Standing upright and shifting to look at his brother eye to eye, Peter smiles. "Well, I'll tell you what, dear brother. If you will take hold of part of this net and help me out, the time will go faster, and the moment will arrive sooner."

They are sitting around a table. In its center a small oil lamp glows brightly, its otherwise stately presence dancing lightly as its flame responds to the air being moved by a gesture or a bit of laugher.

"So many things to consider," James begins. "So much lies ahead and not that distant."

Jessie studies him. "Well, there is sufficient work, good measure of it, I might add, each day until then."

"You are correct," John responds, "but think of it ... The Promise will unfold! Soon it will become known. I measure not more than two years, and all will know of Him. All these years, all this preparation ..." His voice trails off in speculation. "And where are the others? I have heard naught of late of any activity at the river. Where are John and those with him?"

"In the interior," Jessie answers. "No one really knows why, but there is no question that they are about something, that John is teaching them that which they will need for the times just ahead. So many of them, as you well know, my brothers, did not received the gifts that we did."

The predawn dampness is chilled by the slow-moving wind. It is audible, but barely so. Nathanael stands leaning upon his glistening staff, eyes scanning the horizon as the entrée of the light casts curious, majestic shadows of color and light. As he turns, his body reacts to the past encounters wherein he had taken a blow. A sharp pain runs up his side, and he gasps aloud, clutching his great staff, his hands and knuckles whitening under the pressure of his grasp. He can no longer stand and falls to one knee as his head slumps forward. "My Lord," he calls out, "it is I, Thy servant Nathanael. Dost Thou call me?"

Again and again the pains course through his body. His left arm falls from the staff to his side, useless, limp. Though his face is twisted with the growing pain, yet are his eyes bright and shining, reflecting the predawn light like two tiny mirrors of perfection, and he speaks with a gentle sweetness. "Ah, my Lord, you do call me. I struggle to free myself from the garb of finiteness. Give me but a moment, Lord, and I shall be free, but I must first bless them before I depart."

He begins a soft, barely audible prayer in the sort of singsong chant typical of the warrior priests called guardians. We hear him call the names of all those his heart and arms have embraced, and we see the vision as he projects it forward in his prayer. It is a collage of memories of joyful times and moments of service.

Finally, he looks up. "I am ready, Lord."

Slowly, as though unseen hands gently cradle his great form, his body comes to rest comfortably upon the knoll where he kept the watch, and his right hand brings to his side the glistening staff that had so long served him as a guardian in service to the Promise.

Armor and weaponry clatter as the soldiers march out the main gate. Group by group they advance, the predawn's light glistening off their highly polished *accoutrements*. Along the sides and to the forefront are mounted soldiers who are of higher stature.

"Where do they go, such a great number?"

"I know not," Miriam whispers to Jeremiah, "but we must strive to discover this. There is something taking place, and it cannot be but trouble for our people."

They move quietly though the side streets and along the narrow passageways between the structures, pausing here and there to greet some whom they know casually, offering small bags of herbs for sale to others who are passing by. This is their custom, a form of service, or merchandizing, by way of which they are able to interact with travelers and everyone, even the legions themselves. For it is known that these peoples and those who are the brethren of that one who is called Prophet, meaning the Forerunner, can heal, doing wondrous works unto almost any need.

They meet up with the others. James' face is tense with concern. "How did the word get out?"

"That I do not know," Jeremiah answers, "but Miriam and I have heard much from many different groups. So it appears to be widely known. Perhaps it is one of the sailors, or a merchant. Who knows? It matters not, really. What does matter is that they are looking for Him."

"Do they know what they are looking for?"

Glancing at Miriam, Jeremiah turns back to James. "Not specifically, so I guess you could say, no. But they are looking for anything unusual."

"Well, to where do they journey at this point?"

"We heard from a guard at the gate who favors her," Jeremiah laughs softly, returning his glance to Miriam who looks away, her face flushed. "We heard that they are going to search in several directions. Which is why they are of such a sizable company … some to the north, some to the seacoast, and what concerns me most is that some are being dispatched to the south, southwest."

James glances at his brother John, and then over to Nathanael, the younger who has come to join them.

Nathanael speaks quietly. "The Master travels south towards Alexandria. Others of our company have traveled to the southwest where the soldiers are headed. But that was a time passed. I am sure that they are secure. And the guardians will see them long before they present a danger."

James and John nod in affirmation.

"But," Miriam counters softly, "I think they will seek out John first and those with him." She strikes her heart thrice.

"The Master always said, it is not the dis-ease that you are seeking to help them be free of, but the seed which has borne it into reality." John pats the trunk of the tree under which they have paused. "Just as with this tree, you must find its root, and therein do you find that which is sufficient to give birth unto the fruit. It matters not whether you consider this literally; the fruit represents something of goodness, for every dis-ease offers the opportunity for goodness."

"How can this be?" one of the newcomers asks.

"Because as it comes to pass that you are there with one of dis-ease, you can bring the goodness of God, and with the power that you have in your heart through your belief, and on occasion ..." John pauses to tap his side, where it is widely known he has a goodly store of tiny pouches containing various herbs, "on occasion with the help of some of these." He pats the side of his overcoat.

"In whose name do we speak the words?" Lamosa asks.

"There is only one God," John says gently but directly, "and there is but one messenger of that one God. He is our elder Brother, the Christ, the Promise of God. In His name, as He has given it unto me and many of my brothers and sisters, and charged us, *As I give this unto thee, my good brother John, so do I charge you to give it unto others who would receive it, and I give it with thee unto them.*

"So on the morrow, we shall all gather by the river, and we shall cleanse ourselves of that which would tend to limit, distract, or create the illusion. The water of life borne in the river as the Spirit of God giving life to this world shall give life to you, too, and if you believe, it will be given to you for eternity."

The differing scrolls in a splendid variety of forms and woven fabrics are wondrous to behold. There are many, all grouped in small areas here and there to represent the varying lands and teachings.

The four priests are studying with adepts of the School who have come from the lands and speak the tongues of these scrolls. As the adepts translate the writings, the inscriptions, the diagrams, and more, the priests nod and annotate their own scrolls in languages that are agreed upon to hold the sacred teachings of all time.

One priest is scrutinizing a beautiful multi-colored diagram. The Master is seated to his right, with Elob, Zelotese, and Marta to his left. "Wondrous," murmurs the priest. "It takes all of our teachings all the way back to the beginning and puts them in picture form." He leans forward to open the scroll a bit more. "Look here ... the beginning of consciousness, and here ... the movement of consciousness throughout all that has gone before. And here, see this? Abram, the Messenger of God. And here is David, and from this, the many spires of light indicating the paths of the tribes of our people. And over here are your people." He turns to look at several of the Essenes who are seated, as ever, just behind the Master. His eyes connect with the Master's as he continues, "And here, here are You, my Lord."

Having already studied these during the years of His travel, and having spoken with those who were the guardians of these sacred teachings, Jesus knows them well. Leaning forward with graceful ease, as the priest studies Him carefully, the Master extends His arm and runs His forefinger along the main line, a lifeline, it could be called, of the entire scroll, pointing to special places indicated with diagrams and symbols in diverse tongues. "And here you are, my brother, and your teachings, and those who have gone before you. I say unto you, what you see here is you. You are the fruit of the tree of your own spirit, born into this life that you could take these gifts," running his finger down the main line of the diagram, "and bring them to this point, here." His finger moves to and from the point the priest had just indicated in reference to Him. "And here are we. See? Where the lines come together from the many diverse places is where we are now." He raises His hand. "And all of you are a part of it."

The priest, watching, listening carefully to Jesus, becomes illumined with inner joy, which radiates from his smile. He closes his eyes and begins to bob forward and back just a bit, striking his chest as he offers prayers to all of the ancient ones of whom he has knowledge.

"We must find them, to warn them," Judas vows quietly.

"Why us?" Phillip asks.

"Because we are not so well known in connection with the others. We will raise far less concern, be less noticeable. And you have traveled this way a lot, my brother, so it is normal, and that is what we need."

Phillip nods, and they continue on.

A bit more to the south, another small group moves slowly, but with a steady pace as they search for their brothers and sisters whom they believe to be in the outlands. Hopeful to find the whereabouts of John and their brothers and sisters accompanying him, they travel this way and that, like tiny fingers of light.

All the while, John and the group have returned to the river and begun their ceremony of initiation of the newcomers … those who will answer the Call, and those who will travel and do works according to the word of the Master.

A considerable outcry swells as the other guardians bear Nathanael's body to the main encampment near the Three Holy Mountains, by the sea.

Herbs, spices, and garments are quickly prepared, as the Holy Maidens gather in a circle with Nathanael at its center.

Some of the other brothers have gone up the hillside to prepare a cavern in which he will be placed to rest.

Younger sisters who are initiates have begun to prepare the scrolls of testimony to honor Nathanael and his deeds ... to tell of his service on the eve of the Master's entry into the Earth, to tell of his service by the great sea in warding off that which would seek to quell the light of hopefulness now illumined in the Earth.

On the same eve that his body is prepared, the great ceremony, prayer, and special anointing are held. Flanking the long carrier that holds his body, the remaining guardians kneel shoulder to shoulder, their heads bowed, looking down upon the form of their brother.

None speak, but all of the Expectant Ones can hear the silent prayer in their own hearts.

And their spirits rejoice in celebration of Nathanael's birth into life beyond.

The Holy Maidens have gathered by the great Healing Spring, as is their custom. Some, eyes filling with tears yet again, lovingly recount their experiences with their brother Nathanael.

Abigale talks about the time Nathanael, the younger, was brought in by his namesake and how her heart leapt for joy at the sight of him, and again when the guardian Nathanael granted him the great honor, the gift of his own name.

Her eyes somewhat unfocused as she stares at the top of the Spring's small pool of water, Andra turns to her sisters and begins to laugh softly. "Do you remember that time when Nathanael, the elder, came upon our group here," and she laughs again, "and we were purifying ourselves? Do you remember his face?" They all begin to laugh.

"Oh, yes," Zephorah recalls with a chuckle. "He was so embarrassed. I do not think we saw him for three days afterwards. Even though we were but children, he could not look at us."

Hannah, too, chuckles. "I know, and the elder sisters laughed and laughed to have a guardian come upon us in our purification ritual. I imagine it is a mark that he must still carry." She looks up. "Wherever you are, bless you, brother." She gestures to the brightly lit evening sky.

"Oh, my … This is what it will be like."

"What do you mean, Little Mary?" Eloise asks.

She pauses. "When our elder Brother leaves us, this is what it will feel like."

As though someone had clamped a large inverted bowl over them, all sound and movement seem to cease as each one uniquely visits that time ahead when the Master called Christ shall, according to the prophecy and His honoring of it, depart the Earth.

Shaking herself as though from a trance, Little Mary glances at each of the Holy Maidens, older now, and smiles. "But there are many beautiful works between now and then, and many joyful times of being able to see the truths we awakened in Him, which He has so beautifully woven into oneness with the Light of God, and which have become His own light that He now gives to the world."

Many of the Maidens sigh deeply, their faces transfixed with wonder and enchanting smiles of love and peace.

Abigale smiles upon each of her Sisters. "And so it is for us to hold this joy now at the moment of His departure, and thereafter. We know we hold truths in our hearts and we know that this journey is but one of many." She stretches out her arms to the others. "In our remembrance of each of us holding Him, rocking Him in our arms as a babe, giving Him and all the others from our hearts and from the golden cup within that which we are and have to give, let us sing. Let us sing and rejoice right now … for our brother Nathanael born into the life eternal, for our Brother Jesus, and for all of our brothers and sisters who are out there right now …" she gestures with a wide sweeping motion of her arm, "preparing for the Promise to be made manifest. Let us sing, my Sisters, and fill our hearts, our minds, and this sacred ground with the joy of our faith."

With that, she begins to softly, rhythmically, clap her hands and sway to the left, and the right, and back, and back again, as she sings tenderly, her clear, sweet voice floating on the night. The other Holy Maidens laugh and giggle as they, too, begin to clap and sway and sing, the sweetness of their song of hope reverberating across the terrain.

On the other side of the great stream … the Sacred Spring, flowing downward as though gifting the Earth with the sweet freshness of the waters of life … one can perceive, if they have eyes to see, the shadowy luminous forms of the Ancient Ones, gathered arm in arm in great circles of light, dancing in the song of joy that is the Promise of God.

If you look into your own heart you will find therein a guardian ... some aspect of your own being that is ever at the ready, that bears only love and compassion as its intention to give in the Earth, yet holds on to the truth and honor of God so that the balance of these wondrous polarities shall become manifest as the Rod of God, called Righteousness.

As you cleave unto this, the joy of the Promise of God will come forth. Whatever you must give of self unto that which comes before you, whether in challenge or in petition, give it. For by so doing, greater will be given unto you.

Chapter Twelve

𝕴𝖙 𝕳𝖆𝖘 𝕭𝖊𝖌𝖚𝖓

The drumming creates a curious effect. Rhythmic, mellow, not harsh, its cadence seems to call to something deep within one's spirit, one's soul. The Master is watching peacefully, joyfully, as those of the School who are from the East, the Persians, perform their ceremonial dance to the rhythm of the drummers who are one with them. Occasionally the Master sways with the rhythm, smiling as He perceives the spirit being manifested in one or more of these Children of God who are performing their ceremony in honor of God's very Name.

Other activities take place that celebrate the preservation of those truths that are known to be the call of righteousness, that for those who shall come forward in times ahead and seek them, these that have been preserved shall be here at the ready and can serve their intent and their awakening.

His body now aged and moving less easily, Jacob sits watching the sizable gathering participate in the various events, a time that has been foretold and long anticipated. There is an air of rebirth and renewal, and he drinks it in as he also drinks in the essence of the Master, seated beside him.

Jacob's eyelids flutter closed for a moment or two as he recalls a time long past when he was atop a large boulder and began to celebrate the dawning of a new day, dancing, singing, and finally reaching down to grasp the hand of young

Jesus who was standing atop John's shoulders. Jacob's face breaks into a smile. When his eyelids flutter open, he turns. His eyes meet the warm, loving gaze of the Master, who has been studying him.

"Those were joyful times," the Master whispers. "I, too, hold them here." He places His hand over His heart. "And I say this to you, my sweet brother Jacob … Ever shall they be the foundation upon which the truth of the Promise can rest securely. And in any time of need or challenge, thou art with me here." He taps His chest.

Exchanges of this sort continue between the two. During an appropriate pause, Zelotese leans forward to look at Jacob and smile, recognizing Jacob's immense part in what is being celebrated before them. He then turns to the Master. "When shall it begin? Do you know?"

The Master is now looking at a number of others who have gathered about them here, His eyes glazed over with a strange light. One could perceive it as a reflection from the various ceremonial fires, but Jacob and Zelotese know it is the light of the Spirit of God, ready to express itself through this, the Son of God.

For a time, He simply appears to be in a blissful state. Finally, His face bathed in sweet serenity, the Master turns to Zelotese and extends an arm across his shoulders. "Very soon, my brother. And let me give of my heart to you for the many gifts we have received from you and your brethren here, and for preserving the truth, and for all else, far beyond expression, that you have given."

They lean to touch their heads together for a moment.

Then in a swift graceful motion, the Master rises to His feet and brings His arms up.

In but a moment, all become quiet. Smiling, looking at this man, they listen with heart, mind, and spirit.

"My Father, it is I. Look You through mine eyes unto these." He turns ever so slowly to look upon and embrace each one present, receiving in return a smile of equally loving warmth and profound understanding. "See, My Father, the joys of my heart. That which I have to give, multiply it. As I now give it to them, let Thy eternal Spirit rest upon each one, and may each ever walk in the peace of the power of Thy Name." He brings His hands together and bows His head. All present do likewise.

"Why do we continue into the wilderness? What is our destination?"

Turning to look at the young adept, John answers with a smile, "The destination is to discover ourselves."

"Is it a place?"

"Perhaps so." Still smiling, he adds, "But then, that is for you to decide."

"How would I make this decision?"

"That, Samuel, you must discover. That, indeed, is the purpose of the journey."

A soft chuckle comes from Iliam, who at John's side.

John continues to stride strong, long, measured paces, as though he were following a predetermined path.

Finally, as they come to a small hollow and rest, Samuel returns again. "Lord, we thirst."

Casually lounging on an upslope behind him, John turns to look at the group that has followed them, considerably more than a score. His mind wanders briefly as he ponders what lies ahead for these whom he shall send to walk with and serve the Promise.

After a time, his eyes return to rest on Samuel. Jessie has moved up to sit beside him, smiling. John looks at her and notices that her lips are parched. He looks around. Signs of everyone's thirst are evident, but there is no concern. He turns his head to glance at Iliam who simply smiles and, finally, shrugs his shoulders, as though some inaudible interchange just took place between them.

Rising, John strides to the center of the group and turns 'round and about. "I am told by young Samuel that he has thirst. Is it so for any of the rest of you?"

They quickly look with curiosity at one another and then at John, for is it not evident, they think, that he would know of their need?

"Come, let us join together then in prayer and meditation, in oneness with God, and what we need shall be given us." Without waiting for a response, he sits down, and Iliam comes over to sit just off to his left. John begins to offer a quiet prayer and then starts to rock his body, just a bit.

Iliam, though his eyes are closed, performs identical movements.

After a long pause, we hear John say, "Wheresoever thou art, whatsoever might befall thee, if ye ask it in His Name, it will be given unto thee. Believe unto this, and thy way shall be made aright. Deny it, and thou art lost." It is difficult to measure the time that passes, for in such a state time is an illusion.

The abruptness of the loud sound as John claps his hands startles some, but not his long-standing brothers and sisters. Looking into the sky, he walks over to one of the young maidens and extends his hand. "Sweet maiden, give me some bread."

All search one another's faces quickly, for not only are they without water, but their food is nearly gone as well. Yet unhesitatingly, she reaches for a loaf and hands it to John.

He leans over and touches her forehead as he whispers, "Faith is a very good thing."

Turning, he strides up the hillside to stand atop a dune. The view of desolation could be wearying to some, burdensome to the spirit. But not to John. His hands are up.

Clasped in one is the loaf. He turns this way and that.

Soon the others, having followed John's line of sight, can see what apparently he knew was there.

A great winged creature begins a slow, spiraling decent. From a distance, it appears that the creature will land atop John. Several of the new adepts look at each other with concern. Finally, it comes to rest and bounces across the short distance to stand before him.

Holding the loaf behind him, John bends and speaks. No one can hear the words, but they do hear a bit of laughter. He breaks a morsel from the loaf and holds it out. The great bird takes it and bounces a few paces away. Above, they can see another, perhaps the mate of this one, circling.

John gives more bread to the creature, then kneels and bows his head. Hands outstretched, he gives the entire loaf to the bird.

In a swift, graceful motion, it takes flight again, soaring mere meters above the surface of the terrain, swooping up and down, circling over those who accompany John. After reaching a certain height, it begins a slow, lazy, flapping movement. John gestures for all to follow him. Without another word, he turns and follows in the direction of the great creature.

The group rushes to follow him. On and on they travel, trying to keep up with him. Finally, they see John stop atop a ridge before them. Many are weary, near to the point of exhaustion.

He stands looking away from them. Then his hands rise once more. To the group's utter shock and amazement, he begins to sing and dance, his hands still up, turning about in little circles, clapping, leaning this way and that. Finally, he turns to look at the group and laughs vigorously. "Come, my brothers and sisters." He extends his arm and points down beyond the ridge. "Come, satisfy your thirst."

Far below the ridge he stands upon, the winged creature can be seen bouncing along the edge of a beautiful pool of water. Surrounding trees sway gently in the mid-day wind, an abundance of dates and other fruits hanging sumptuously, ready for harvest by John and his followers.

Their fires are warming them. Their thirst and hunger have been satisfied and their bodies purified by the cool waters of the spring.

Now, near the edge of night, they see John standing alone, looking off into the distance. Atop a distant dune, they see something moving.

Silently, John raises a hand.

A chill runs through them as they hear the call of a desert lion. Then, several others of the pride appear and sit looking down upon the scene.

John kneels to offer a silent prayer, and as gently and swiftly as they appeared, they vanish.

He rises again and walks to the farthest edge of the campfire's light. Peering across the dunes, he bows his head, asking softly, "Art thou with God?"

Naught but Iliam hears this, for, as so oft, he is only a pace or two away.

In the inner chambers of sacred light within John's heart, we hear, *I am with God.*

Hearing within the inner recesses of his being the voice of a beloved guardian called Nathanael, John strikes his chest and without a word, Iliam does likewise. "I shall miss the sight of thee," John speaks aloud.

Moments pass in the silence of the night's embrace and we hear yet another voice. *Be of good cheer, brother John. The time is nigh. It is well for you now to return to the river, and let the Word be made manifest.*

"Who art thou that speakest such to me?"

I am he who is ever with thee.

"Art thou Shem?"

That is I. Take thy rest, brother, for He comes!

"How wonderful to be together again. I have so missed

being with you." Mary looks about the circle of Her beloved Sisters.

Andra asks gently, "How have you fared, my Sister?"

"It has been a long ... one might say, empty journey, in a way. The absence of my beloved, who was not only husband, but also friend and teacher, is a great void. And yet, in dream and vision ..." She looks around to smile, for all remember Her as a child talking about the Spirit of God spilling down all over Her. "It is the light of Joseph now that embraces me. But enough. What of each of you? I have heard so much. James and John have been active, have they not?" She turns to look at Jessie and Moira, who have joined the group.

"They are active, all right." A bit of humor lies just beneath the surface of Hannah's response.

"And John?" Mary questions Hannah with a smile.

She answers wistfully. "Soon the Sisters and I will go to join him."

"It is to begin soon, then?" Rebekah asks, fully knowing the answer, but feeling that verbalizing it will somehow soften what they know must come.

"It is very near unto the time." Mary's eyes soften, Her gaze seemingly transfixed on something invisible, which every Sister feels and knows, for they are one.

"Cast off all that binds you. Set aside whatever distracts you. Repent from that which has been, and claim that which can be. The Lord God does not punish you for wrongdoing. That which is, is done unto you by you."

"How so?" questions one in the throng gathered at the river's edge. "The Romans come and take what they would from my house. I do not do this unto myself. They do it!"

John focuses upon this one. "Do you not hear the truth of my words? If you look beyond that which seems to be, you will find the answer to your question. But so long as you cling to that which is known and familiar, so will it become that which you experience, that which is you. Go within yourself. Find that place which is your strength, your truth, and call it forth. For in the light that shines from within, all things are possible, all things can be known. But unless you strip away that to which you cling from habit, that which is the greater within can never be seen!

"So do I say to you, cast these off. Repent from that which is habitual and joyfully go forward into that which calls to thee. Come you here. Stand with me in this river of God's Spirit. And in the Name of that one greater than I, who is soon to come, together we shall cleanse your mind, your heart, your spirit, that you can be anew … that you can step forth from this river and, as you will it, be born again."

Something within one frail-looking man seems to drive him forward. As though he is outside of himself watching curiously, he moves into the water, now up to his waist.

"Give me your hand, my brother," John requests.

Robotically, the man places his hand, thin and frail, in John's strong, beautiful one.

"Know this," John begins gently, "thou art greater than that which you seem. Look you. See your hand in mine? The Promise, which is to come, is with me in Spirit here. It is in His Name, that of my Brother Jesus, that I call upon the Lord God to awaken His Light within you and free your spirit."

The man begins to tremble. His lip quivers. "I have such sadness within me."

"This I know. Here in my hand is the hand of the Grace of God given in the Name of the Christ. Take it. I give it unto thee." He extends his hand to take the man's other hand. "Let this be as a circle of the living Light of God coursing through us, brother to brother."

The man's head slumps and he begins to sob.

In an easy, gentle motion, John moves to embrace him, rubbing his back, speaking softly. "Let that which has limited and burdened you be free. Send it forth like a great bird and let the Light within grow and shine all through you, and you shall become transformed. For the gifts of God await you. But you ... and only you ... can claim them."

The man looks up into John's eyes, and what he sees he knows is truth, eternal Truth. "Heal me. Cleanse me."

Reaching within his outer coat, John pulls forth his bowl and baptizes him.

The warmth of the sun seems to penetrate the crispness in the air. As the sparkle of the clear water gently passes by John, who is standing not quite midstream, he peers into the distance, in expectation, wonder, and love. The light which emanates from there is sufficient to part the group of Holy Maidens and all the brothers and sisters gathered before John, previously listening to his prayers and his teachings.

The figure strides, with confidence and surety, unto the water's edge, and the two brothers move to embrace one another, according to their individual and group destiny. The Master's answer to the question John poses to Him affirms His commitment to the path ahead, tempered and strengthened through the purification ritual, that its spirit will endure any labors that might be required.

At the moment of the Master's emergence, the light of heaven transcends and shines upon Him and upon John, as well. In the unification of the forces borne through the Baptist and borne through the will of the Master as Jesus, comes the merging of the spirit of the Christ with the man Jesus: His final stage of initiation, the final purification process, and the emerging of that which is to be the living, eternal example.

The odors are foul and the stifling air barely moves. There is the smell of hatred, even of death.

"Someone is here to see you, Prophet!" a guard growls.

John, seated against a wall on a bit of straw, looks past the guard to see the warm, smiling face of Iliam.

"Be brief," the guard cautions. "I could have troubles for doing this, great ones, which all the coin you could give me would not solve."

The door thuds shut, and Iliam walks in. Without looking at John, he walks about, hands behind his back, looks up towards the top of a wall where there are some bars with a bit of light shining through. Finally, he turns to look at John. "Nice quarters."

John throws his head back and laughs robustly, then he, too, glances around. "Well, I have seen better, but this will do. Come, join me. I have naught to offer you, save the bread of life within." He chuckles softly.

"Well, I do!" Iliam reaches within his outer coat and pulls out a small flask and a loaf. "Let us celebrate, my brother."

John rearranges his legs and sits up. "You gladden my spirit. Yes, let us celebrate."

So, in the traditional Essene manner, they make their prayers and offerings. They remember all those who have gone before, calling them out name by name. They remember the ancient ones and honor them. Then, they break the bread, calling it the Bread of Life, and each gives unto the other that which they have taken from the loaf. They partake of the bread and the wine, then move into prayer and meditation. In mere moments, their spirits come together and soar off into the light, laughing, joyful.

"They have taken him," Nathanael-the younger quietly informs Jesus.

Jesus responds not, but looks off into the distance.

Jessie, Moira, Hannah, Rebekah, and so many of the others are gathered with the Master one last time at the great Healing Spring.

All are silent at the news from Nathanael, the younger.

The Master turns to Rebekah. "How did he fare upon my

awakening and departure?"

Rebekah, clinging to Hannah's hand, looks up at Jesus, the brightness of her spirit shining through. "My Sister and I tended him until he was strong, and he began his journey, knowing, of course, that it would lead to where he is now."

"And he was well?" the Master asks.

"Yes," Hannah responds, "only asking of my Sister and me that we tell you that his spirit is ever with you and the Promise."

The Master simply nods and looks down, brushing the pebbles and soil on the earth before Him.

Then, with His right hand He scoops up a handful and holds it up. As he loosens His grasp on it, the soil begins to trickle from the bottom of His hand back to the ground. "We are as this," He speaks softly. "Each grain of sand, each pebble, of itself is of no great significance." He opens His hand and it all returns to the ground before Him. "Notice, though," He glances about, "together the many grains of sand make the Earth upon which we now rest."

He nods in the direction of the small stream of water coming down into the pool of the Healing Spring. "Each drop unto itself is minute, but together is that which can give life."

There is a prolonged silence. A stillness.

The Master turns and looks at all His beautiful brothers and sisters. "So are we, and so is our brother John, as that ... the Healing Spring ... as this, the very Earth upon which we rest, for he wishes it to be such." He turns to look at Nathanael. "I am with him. Though my body is here, I am ever with him."

"Why do you chain me?" he asks boldly.

"Because thou art a prisoner."

"Do you see a purpose for these chains?" John raises his hands so that they can be seen.

"Of course! Has your mind left you already, before your

head does?"

"These chains do not bind me. You are only performing that which concludes my flight."

As they guide him along to his destination, John looks about, for there are many here and there in recesses, in alcoves, who are looking upon this Prophet of God, as he has come to be called. Some call out to him, "Call upon your God. Free yourself."

John, shuffling, smiles as he answers, "Look carefully, for I am already free."

"It is important that you keep your spirits bright," Anna counsels quietly, "as you have lived that brightness. As you go forth, know that our hearts, our spirits, journey with you."

"Will you not come with us?" Zephorah's eyes are moist with love for these great teachers.

"As Our Lord has said it, we are always with you," Anna responds tenderly. Judy simply nods.

"But she means we want to have you with us physically," Sophie adds lightly, but with serious intent.

"It has begun," Judy whispers. "All these things you know."

"Yes, I know them," Kelleth interjects, "but I did not know the specifics. I thought you would always be with us, especially now."

"No, it is time that you must go, all of you."

"What will you do, sweet sister?" Hannah asks.

"We will complete our journey. And look you," Judy points down the slope to where groups of children are playing and singing, "we have a bit more to do with these young ones."

"As I look upon them, my heart sings, yet a part of me grieves." Little Mary works to hold back her tears. "Sweet sister, sweet teacher, help me with my sorrow. Help me cast it aside. I know its nature. Why does it keep visiting me?"

With considerable effort, Judy rises to make her way across the space separating her from Little Mary. One can almost feel the effort required as she bends to kneel. Straightening her outer garment, she takes Little Mary's face in her hands and pulls her forward to kiss her upon the forehead before reaching down to take her hand. "Whensoever such grief or sorrow visits thee, do this," she brings Little Mary's fingertips up to her forehead, "and remember me, and remember my kiss, for you and I are ever one. All of us, sweet sisters … We are the hope. We are that which gives birth to what can be. Build upon what has been and visit it often in celebration and joy, not in the garb of sorrow or remorse, lest that be what goes before you."

Rising, she takes her sister Anna's hand, and they stand together in the circle of sisters and others.

"His work has begun, Anna begins. "The journey is brief, but eternal. He will look to you … in His Spirit and physically, resting His eyes upon each of you.

"As one who thirsts goes to a well to drink, give unto His need whenever He asks, and give in joy. Let not sorrow, but joy, go before you, that in His moment of need and coming unto you, you meet that, and you give your hopefulness, your expectancy, your love, your compassion, and all the truths that have been woven into the oneness which has become the Promise of God."

"Where is John now?" Nicodemus asks quietly.

"Captured."

Nicodemus bows his head and strikes his chest. "Then it has in truth begun?"

"Yes, it has, as you say, begun."

"What of the Maidens and the others?"

"They are now journeying to join Him."

Nicodemus is filled with emotion. Seeing him struggle, several of his aides come to his side, but he waves them away. "No, I must know this. I must feel it. I must become one with it. For that which lies ahead will call upon the greatest within each of us, and I, Nicodemus, shall not be found wanting."

"May I take my leave of you?" Justus asks respectfully.

Glancing at him and young Nathanael, Nicodemus nods, smiling. "A moment." He gestures to his servants to bring food and stores to sustain them. "I suspect you journey to find the Master?"

Young Nathanael looks down, clearly impacted by the loss of his brother John. "It was his wish for us to so do. And so it is a parting, in no small measure a longing, to be with him again. And yet, we rejoice, as he encouraged us, and are eager to be one with Jesus and the Work."

"Take these, then." Nicodemus thrusts stores into their hands, wrapped in simple-looking woven bags. "When you see Him, would you say this unto Him …"

"Anything, as you wish it," Justus answers.

"Say to Him … Thy brother, Nicodemus, prays that the peace of God ever be upon Thee.'"

✦

In each journey, dear friends, there is a point at which you begin and another at which you end.

The measure of each journey is not so much where you begin and where you end, but how you have traveled. None can measure this for you, in truth. They can see and speak unto it, gladly offering the reflections of their good intentions for you, but only you can measure your journey, and the joy that is its harvest.

If there is that within you which is bur-dened, belabored, remorseful, sorrowful, or grief-stricken at what will be, then not only is that future time lost, but its shadow takes away the now, as well.

Thus, ever strive to let joy shine forth in who and what you are, and on your journey. As John spoke to his captors, say unto your-selves, as well, that nothing can bind you, if, in truth, your spirit is free.

What lies ahead is the beginning of the Hope of God ... yes, the very Hope of God: that the Children of God shall be about their journeys in the intention of His joy for them.

Chapter Thirteen

The Promise Is Awakened

The priests are gathered in somewhat nervous anticipation. "Well, give us a report, Captain. What is the result of your sorties?"

"I will give you a report, but first, let me ask, what idiot took the head of the Prophet? No one will speak to us. They spit and throw stones at us! We are under siege here in the city and all the little villages. This was unquestionably the action of one who has lost all reason!"

"Mind your tongue, Captain," another priest whispers.

"I tell you, there is no point in sending us forth again like this, unless you know the specific whereabouts of the Zealots or any of the other rebels. It is pointless. No one, I tell you, no one will speak, no matter how much coin we offer, no matter what boons we present to them. You can see it in their eyes, their faces. There is nothing but hatred towards us."

One of the head priests looks at the other two with intense, confused emotion. "I told you! See? It begins. It will be our downfall!"

"Speak not those words, Lamechus!" the priest on the left retorts. "For in the spoken word is the potential. I will hear you speak of such things no more."

This has little impact upon the third priest, and the scorn and array of emotions passing through him are visible, for he is not without his own inner visions and guidance. And what he perceives … no, what he feels … is his own demise.

"I returned to say these things to you in person," Iliam informs his brothers and sisters who are gathered at the great School. "This shall be my last visit here," he gestures, arms outstretched, "and perhaps the last time my physical eyes will behold you, brothers and sisters. It is appropriate that I come to tell you that the Promise is awakened and unfolding."

Many look at one another and whisper back and forth. Some show their spiritual impact with gestures, signs and salutations.

To the rear, left, and right of the group, soft drumming begins.

Iliam looks at the drummers who smile and nod. "Thank you, my brothers. I know whereof you drum."

He cannot continue, and bows his head for a moment.

Glancing up at the top of Reflection Rock, Iliam turns and speaks in a loud clear voice. "Would you honor me and our brother John in a moment of prayer."

Word has reached the more distant settlements, many of which were often frequented by the Desert Prophet, as he was often called by those humble peoples. Some have begun to prepare goods and such, for word has gone forth that a ceremony will be held at the river's edge.

The Maidens are encircled by the remaining guardians and some of the younger company who have rejoined the main tribe for this time of the Awakening. Some of the elders are carried by animals or by litter. It is a sizable group. No matter what might be done, it is impossible to conceal it, so their normal care or caution is not as prevalent, indeed, seems all but absent.

As they move through small herding and similar villages en route to the river, many followers come to line their pathway. Some hurry to their simple huts and reemerge with small bundles, falling in behind to accompany the large group. Then come those who are from the distant western reaches and from the cities. And so it grows.

Finally, the goodly numbers merge here at the river's edge, while great filamentary clouds move lazily across the sky in anticipation of the coming rain.

Close to the river's edge on a slight outcropping Jesus and His disciples (those whom He has approached and to whom He has spoken the words, Follow me) are seated.

Toward the west and south, and somewhat from the north, there is higher ground, sloping gently down to where the Master sits on the rock abutment. He looks around at the group. Nearby are those who once walked with John, as well as those who have come from the various tribes to begin their part, as agreed, to support and nurture the Promise of God. Scattered around the periphery, watching, looking, are the few remaining guardians. They have begun this phase of their sacred work of preserving both the Master and His teachings.

Speaking unto His followers, the Master offers words softly, gently. Several of the disciples and those with them ask Him diverse questions.

Thaddeus, his face aglow with anticipation, asks, "O Lord, is this the day? The beginning?"

Jesus looks about the remainder of the group whose up-turned faces are bright and hopeful. He pauses to study Peter carefully and smiles, for He can see in this one's heart the stalwartness, the courage, the willfulness of his soul.

He comes upon the eyes of Judas who brings his hands to his heart and then up to God, symbolizing in the Essene manner: I give thanks in my heart unto God for your presence. Jesus smiles and nods. Very slowly, He places His hand over His heart, then brings it to His lips, placing a kiss upon it and giving it to Judas by way of His outstretched hand. As the sun glances off a particularly majestic cloud, a reflected ray of sunlight strikes Jesus on His upper body, illuminating Him.

Those nearby can see a tear.

Only then does Jesus turn away from Judas and answer, "This, my brother, is an ending and a beginning, both. For in order that the House of God be built, we must lay this foundation of faith firmly in place, and we must honor it. That what I am to give can be built upon the faith of John."

The Holy Maidens are gathered at the river's edge. They form a small, semi-circular line and sway this way and that, singing, their faces luminous. In the center is Our Lady Mary, who is the first to step forth. Reaching into Her outer garment, She pulls forth a small packet, a bit of cloth folded delicately. One can see the care of workmanship upon it and a bit of bright-colored ribbon made from special herbs and inks brought from the east and given to Her by Zelotese.

Lifting Her outer garments, Mary steps into the water and looks up. Her face is aglow with the sweetness of God. She speaks naught, but all know what is said from Her heart.

Carefully, delicately, She places the small packet on the surface of the water and releases it, straightening Herself to watch as the slow movement of the river's current carries it out to mid-stream as it spins and moves. She nods, smiling. She gestures first to Her heart, to Her lips, to Her head, and then outward and upward to God. "I release thee, my brother. The peace of God be upon thee."

So it proceeds. Each Maiden comes forth, some bearing items made of wildflowers, others simple but meaningful little mementos that remind them of all the joy, the wondrous works they have shared with one another from childhood on to bring forth these who are a part of the Promise of God. And now, this action, indeed, this celebration, brings it into the Earth.

Finally, Mary turns and looks up to where Jesus has been standing, observing each one who has given tribute and closure to the foundation of the Work, as He has called it. Mary nods and He reciprocates with a gentle nod and smile.

All of the Maidens are now by Mary's side, their hands to their hearts.

Slowly, Jesus turns to see that not a meter of open ground remains. All of the hillside and river's edge is filled with throngs of peoples. Off in the distance He can even see a sizable gathering of Zealots and He smiles, for He knows that to His brother John, none were strangers. He answered the call, even of the rebel Zealots. He sang with them and supped with them. Jesus knows He must speak to them soon that they shall not seek vengeance on those who have taken the life of one whom they had regarded as a brother.

But for now He feels the import, the majesty, the wonder of the hundreds of upturned faces, and the awesome, stupefying silence, the only sound an occasional breeze in the bulrushes and the tinkling of water falling over a few rocks near river's edge.

"Be thou of good cheer, brothers and sisters," Jesus begins. "For I say unto you, this day one of those of our Lord God's righteous has returned to a place of honor. Let us rejoice and celebrate.

"If there remains sadness," He glances at the group of Zealots, "or anger, remember his works. He would tell you these are those things that can diminish the light of God within you. If yet you have these, come forth unto this river, this place where his work was wrought, and free yourself, as I know he has helped so many of you to become free."

A strong voice comes from the midst of the group to the Master's left, up the slope a bit. "Tell us then. Art thou He? King of our peoples?"

Many turn to look at him quickly. There are murmurs, and the Maidens bow their heads. Two take Mary's arms, Zephorah on Her left and Hannah on Her right. The others stand close by.

"I am that as has been given. He has said it," gesturing to the river, meaning John. "But you must hear it in your own heart and spirit. If I am that as he has given it, then thou shalt see it and know it." The Master turns, and with fluid, measured strides, walks down from the outcropping and begins to walk up the slope towards the northwest.

There is a commotion now, for many cannot believe this. Many are calling out, "Give us a sign." "Give us your teaching." "Drive out the Romans." "Tell us what to do."

The Zealots are yelling, "Take arms. Let us get revenge."

Yet, the Master does not turn back, but continues striding up the hill.

His followers, caught unawares and in disarray, scurry to catch up. Many who are with the disciples and the Master move at a brisk pace, taking up positions on the flank and to the forefront.

Jesus looks up from studying the evening's campfire. His eyes fall upon Miriam, the younger. "Sister, bring unto me, if thou wouldst, yon basin and pitcher of water."

She turns quickly to look in the direction of His gaze. Peering into the pitcher, she quickly takes a water skin, fills it, and brings both it and the basin to the Master, holding them out to Him.

The Master gestures for her to lay them on the ground before Him. Even though many have been talking here and there among the group, all note Miriam's interactions with Him. Those who can see (of which there are many in this company) note the growing light around His body, and they know that what transpires next will be significant.

The Master rises to His knees before the basin. Miriam begins to turn, but He holds His hand up to her. Looking around, He smiles as He sees Jessie and Moira, who blush at the recognition. He gestures to them to come forth. "I would that thou wouldst bathe my head, Miriam, and that thou, sweet sister Jessie, wouldst hold the basin to catch the water as thy sister so does."

Looking straight up at Moira, who stands before Him, He hands her His outer coat. "With this, I ask that you would take the water from me," which is to say, *Dry me.*

All are now riveted. Puzzled, almost all those present have moved closer to see.

"Why does He bathe before us, Thaddeus?"

"I do not think it is mere bathing, Thomas. Look at the Light around Him."

Thomas glances, leaning a bit. His eyes narrow, and then open widely. "You are right!"

"My Father," Jesus prays, looking up, "let these waters be as one with Thy Spirit in Earth made manifest. I open myself unto Thee. Let the spirits of these three, my sisters, bear testimony to that which has been placed within me. Let this action be a gift of gratitude, of thankfulness unto all who have been a part of the journey to this time. All of my sweet Sisters, the Holy Maidens who awakened each gift, who brought forth that rock of truth upon which Thy Truth shall be built, do I bless in this action, that the Waters of Truth bring about the beginning."

He glances at Miriam, and she knows. He bends His head over the basin and closes His eyes. She begins to pour the water over the back of the Master's head.

Mary is seated directly across a considerable expanse, Her arms folded within Her outer coat. Arrayed beside and behind Her are the other Holy Maidens, and to Her either side, those sweet brothers and sisters whose journeys have been so intertwined.

Slowly, the water falls into the basin. When no more remains in the pitcher, there is silence, but for the last few droplets falling from the Master's hair as it hangs down, heavily laden with the Spirit of God.

He brings His head up and looks directly at Moira. Jessie steps back, holding the basin filled to near overflowing with the holy water that has passed over His head. Then Moira, almost unable to accept the great honor, brings the cloth of His outer coat up and gently begins to dry the head of the Christ.

When this is completed, the Master holds His hands up, and Moira, folding His outer coat, places it gently, reverently, in His outstretched hands.

Again He looks up. "Thank You, My Father, for these great blessings, the hands which wove the fibers, having spun them into thread and placed them together with such care, such excellence, and for those who designed the patterns." He names Rebochien, his aides, and others, the seers, prophets and Ancient Ones.

Finally, when His prayer is complete, He looks at Moira, again nodding. She steps forward. He places His outer coat in her arms. "Give this unto our Holy Mother and those with Her. I would that each has a portion of this, so as they seek it, in remembrance of me."

Now, Jessie, who stands with the basin, receives a loving gaze from the Master. "Here, my sweet sister, come. Kneel beside me and place the basin here." And so she does. He looks up. "I would give the Mark of God to those who would receive it. Hear me well. I say unto you, the time is now. That which I give to you is eternal, and all who have eyes to see will see it. With this Mark, I give to thee that which my Father empowers me to give, and that gift is eternal.

"But the way ahead is laborious and to the temple of flesh offers pain and scorn for my sake. Dwell you for a moment in the light of your spirit within that quiet temple wherefrom the voice of God can be heard speaking and guiding you ever. Only then, after you have heard same, come forth, and I will give unto you that Mark of the eternal gift of Spirit and my blessing.

"But if you hear the voice not, then do not fall away in sadness, but know this is not the path for you to walk. If ye have faith, ye will know it to be so, and ye will know also that another path, which is great unto purpose for you, will appear. Seek ye, now."

He settles back upon His knees and heels, hands upon His knees, as He looks about. Many of the group are bobbing, nodding, swaying.

His eyes come to rest on Our Lady, who beams with joy and pride. She smiles and nods at Him, stroking His outer coat, which had been placed upon Her lap. She has swung it up over Her shoulder to cover Her heart, and caresses it, remembering how in a time past, She caressed the small babe who was to be called Jesus.

There is a shuffling sound as the sizable figure of Peter kneels before the Master. "I hear the call, my Lord, and I am come. I will follow Thee unto the ending and beyond, if Thou wouldst have me."

He gazes at Peter, His love and respect for him evident. "Give unto me thy bowl, Peter."

Peter reaches into his outer garment and pulls forth his bowl.

The Master leans forward to take a bit of water from the basin before Jessie, who holds it firmly in place. Holding the bowl outright, He closes His eyes but a moment. "Thou, Peter, art a rock of God, yea even unto that which shall be built, art thou His rock." Dipping two fingers into Peter's bowl of water, the Master anoints him upon the forehead.

Peter's eyes close, fluttering as though some energy were transforming his body.

"The Spirit of God is within thee, Peter. I shall call thee Cephas, the Rock." The Master's hand comes to rest against Peter's cheek.

Peter swiftly raises his hands to clasp it. Barely audible, we can hear Peter say, "My life is yours. I love you."

The Master simply smiles and nods, for He knows full well the love of this man for Him. Yet, He also knows the challenges, the testing, and the purification that lie ahead for this, His brother. And He knows the great pain that Peter will meet when he realizes that all must be left behind, that which is familiar and distant, that which is of fear, doubt, or any such not borne of spirit, but of Earth. He even knows that for this man, evident in the truth borne in his words, a time will come when he shall stand aside.

Several more disciples come forth, and now the Master is looking into the eyes of Judas. His eyes are very large, a curious deep brown color almost like a honeycomb, with little spires of golden hues here and there. They are rounder than some of the others' and filled with the sweetness of his dedication and his honoring of the Prophecy.

The Master extends His hand, but speaks not.

Judas withdraws his bowl from his garments and places it in the Master's hand.

This time, the Master does something different. He places His hand over Judas' that is still holding the bowl. As they bend just a bit to take some water from the basin steadied by Jessie, they do so together.

Judas and Jesus are intertwined in their gazes. "I tell you, my brother, this cup is that which carries the sweetness. It is the pure essence of the Spirit of God that gives the life eternal. There will come a time shortly ahead when that cup I must give unto you will be bitter. In the light of thy spirit's truth, thou knowest this."

Judas blinks, shuddering a bit. "I know of something, Lord, my Master, that lies ahead for me. And I know it is in testimony to the honor we must all hold for God and for your Word. I pledge to you, I will take that bitter cup when it must come to me, and according to the honor of God, which we all hold, so shall I, as He, honor the prophets."

"This I know, my brother. Would that you know this: No thing, nor action, could ever diminish my love for you." He thrusts two fingers into the bowl and places the Mark upon Judas' forehead.

Unlike the previous blessings He bestowed upon the others, He places His hand upon Judas' heart and a kiss upon his forehead.

No more words pass between them. They are unneeded, for the Spirit is the life and the light, and all is known which is of God and is of truth. Within the golden chalice of self, in the silence there, one can know of it. Here, both have done so and affirmed its presence to each other.

He places His Mark and His blessing upon all who come forward, those who will be called Apostles and those who will be recognized as such, but not of sufficient stature to be recorded by name.

The morning sunlight is bright and warm. They have completed their purification, their meal, their rituals, their song. Now, they follow excitedly as the Master strides casually along a road frequented heavily by traders from all destinations. Ahead, He notes several entities seated upon some large rocks off to the left. To the right are some gnarled trees, not great in stature, but sufficient to shelter any traveler from the sun's rays. One can see that many such have rested beneath the shade of these trees.

The Master and those with Him come to a halt. Glancing at the trees and studying the entities off to the left, He looks at them and smiles. They are studying Him and His entourage. "I greet you, good travelers. How fare you?"

The center one, whose beard is great and dark, whose eyes dance and glisten, answers. "We fare quite well. Indeed, very well."

"From whence come ye?"

The man points. "We have completed our trading, and as you can see," he gestures, "we have naught left. We have done very good business these past days."

"Then you are joyful because of your abundance?" the Master asks.

The dark-bearded man throws his head back to laugh the vibrant, merry laugh of someone who is quite comfortable in their way of life. "You could say that. I suppose success and abundance are sufficient cause for joy, would you not agree?"

"It would certainly seem so to look upon you, my brother."

The man effortlessly slides off of the rock on which he has been perched. Straightening his garments, he walks ever so casually over to where the Master stands and extends a hand to Him. "I am called Marcus. And you?"

"I am called Jesus." He gently accepts Marcus' hand, firmly grasping his forearm, as is the custom.

"Hmm …" Marcus strokes his thick beard as he rubs his face. "You know, I have heard tell of you … Yes!" He snaps his fingers. "The Desert Prophet said you would be appearing any day now. How is he? Fascinating fellow!"

Jesus smiles. "He is very well, I assure you. He could be no better."

"Oh, good! So many times he gave us aid, or one of those with him did, and I suppose you could say," looking down he lifts his cloak and continues, "I am one of those examples of his fine work." He extends his leg to show the old wounds where a viper had struck him. "Yes, he changed my life and, as I said, he talked about you. Well, judging from the size of the group with you, I have no doubt you must be He."

Jesus laughs. "Let me ask of you, brother Marcus (he smiles at being called brother), why were you seated upon those rocks where the sun is so vibrant and powerful when over here," He speaks louder so all of His followers nearby can hear Him, "there is the cool, sweet comfort of the shade of these trees?"

Marcus looks at the trees and then back at the rocks. "I suppose it might seem strange to some, but I would think not to you, from what I have heard. We learned that by doing so, to a degree, of course," he smiles and laughs a bit, "we not only bring the power of the sun's light and energy to the body, but we purify it in the process. It is a process which we learned from the Desert Prophet." Marcus laughs again. "This drives out the drosses. It helps the body to become cleansed. And when there is no river or water around," he gestures indicatively, "it is one of the good ways to bathe."

"Then you look upon the sun and such energies, as you called them, as cleansing?"

"Of course." Marcus shrugs, puzzled by the questions.

"You would prefer to endure the intensity of the sun's rays upon your body in order that you might be purified?"

Marcus, strokes his beard again. He pauses briefly, then smiles wholeheartedly. "It would appear so, would it not?"

"Then follow me."

"What?"

"Then follow me. For if you believe unto that which has been given to thee by my brother John and have found it to be good and know it to purge that which impairs or limits, that which creates dis-ease in thy body, then I tell you, if you follow me, I will do the same for your spirit."

Marcus studies Him in utter silence. "I am not of your people. How would you receive me?"

"As this ..." The Master steps forward to embrace Marcus and kisses him upon both of his cheeks.

Something indefinable transpires as the Master embraces this stranger who is a traveler, a merchant, and only He knows what else the man might be.

Tears stream from Marcus. He falls to his knees as the Master steps back. "He said it would be so. He said to be with you is to be as with God. And in your embrace, do I know you. Here." He reaches in both sides of his cloak and pulls out the monies he has only recently received for his labor. "I give this. It is what I have to offer." He places it all at the feet of the Master.

"I have naught else to give. I am not a good man. I am not of any belief, though I do believe in the words of the Desert Prophet, for I saw in them their truth. As my body sees in the sun's light that which can purify it, so did his words and actions, just the same, purify me. But I am not worthy to walk with you. For if thou art in truth He as was spoken of," Marcus looks up, the morning light outlining the silhouette of Jesus looming above him, "then … then you are the Son of God.

"Thou knowest that within is my heart which has not done good, which has, indeed, wronged, though not deliberately, but from need, or the belief in need. But I say to you, here!" He pushes the coins so they fall on the Master's feet. "This is all that I have, and I give it unto you and the Word that you shall bring, as he said it, unto all of the world. But do not take me. I am not worthy. And others will judge you and your Word if they see me present in your good company."

The Master bends and lays His hand on Marcus' head. "Give thy coin, thy wealth, elsewhere, good brother, for I have no need of it. Give it unto the poor. It is naught that I ask of thee to give unto me, my brother, sweet Marcus, for in the center of thy being is the pure Light of God. *I* would give unto *you*. And if you will follow me, together, we will give unto all who ask and are willing to receive."

Sobbing, Marcus falls, grasping the Master's feet, wrapping his strong arms around His ankles and calves, sobbing, rocking, calling out, "Praise God! Praise God!"

The Master lifts him up. "It is not at my feet I wish you, brother, but at my side. What we shall do together in God's Name will bring a gladness, a harvest of abundance to your spirit that is an hundred-fold greater than any such as these," He gently slides the pouches of coin out from before Him. "Welcome, brother."

A withered woman huddles by the side of the village

well. Nearby, two small children in tattered clothing, perhaps ages five to seven, look down but occasionally up to extend a hand outward to any passing travelers. Few, if any, pay the children heed.

The older one looks up to see a group of people walking up the slope to the village square.

The figure at the forefront, striding easily and smiling, seems to be looking back at him. Two come from the group behind Him and trot ahead looking this way and that, stout staffs glistening in the sun's light. Satisfied that there is no danger here, they move off to the sides, and several of the others do the same.

The young lad, Ladocious, jumps to his feet brushing and arranging his garments as best he can, for they are tattered and worn, and trots over to approach the Master, walking, bouncing, dancing backwards, his hands outstretched, asking for coin.

"I have naught coin," Jesus tells him.

"Have you food then? Many are with you. Surely you must have great wealth or they would not all be following you."

"I do have great wealth." The Master has slowed His pace somewhat.

Ladocious falls to His side, and several Apostles come forward, concerned, though they know not why.

The Master glances at them, blinking an okay, of a sort.

"Have you nothing to give me? I am hungry. And look you, my mother has a sickness. She can no longer work. We have no food. We have no coin. We have no place. We stay here under the meager roof of this well, and we have naught. Good sir, can you not give unto us something?"

They are standing a few paces from the well where the woman is crumpled up, covering herself completely with an outer coat. Not even her eyes are visible.

"How are you called?"

"Ladocious."

"What would you have of me? I have already told you I have no coin." He opens His outer coat to show no purse hangs from His sash within.

"Have you no food?"

"I have food," the Master answers softly, "but it is not of fishes and loaves."

Ladocious' mother cracks a fold in the garment covering her head, and those in the forefront see a single eye peering out. It does not look particularly old or dis-eased, but an inexplicable heaviness is about it.

The Master sees this and hears her moan.

She uncovers her face a bit more so both eyes can be seen, and He nods. Her moaning and crying reverberate fully to the rear of the crowd where many of the Master's followers look around, trying to discern what is going on.

Surprisingly, the Master seats Himself on the ground, folding His legs beneath Him and gestures to His followers to gather 'round. He points for Ladocious to sit directly in front of Him. "Give him food and drink, and them, as well."

Several come forward with loaves and dried fishes, and flasks and such, but the young lad refuses the flasks and points to the well instead. Quickly, striving to swallow great mouthfuls of food, Ladocious suddenly stops, and looking at the Master, places the loaves and foods down on a bit of cloth next to him as he raises his hands together in front of him. "Please, forgive me."

The Master smiles broadly. "Thou art forgiven."

The lad shakes his head, "No. I know that thou art a traveler, and you must thirst. Would you give me the honor to draw you water from this well?"

"I would."

Ladocious rises and brings a ladle of cool, clear water to the Master.

"Would you give it unto my brethren, as well?"

The lad looks this way and that way over the top of the Master's shoulders and, seeing the goodly number, sighs.

The Master laughs. "You know not yet of what I speak, do you?"

"Well, good sir, you say to me to give drink to all these people. I am willing to so do, good sir, but it is you that I honor. For you say it, and it is so. See?" He points to his food just a step or two behind him. "When you say the word, then even though you have no coin or food, I look and I say, 'Ladocious, this man's words have great power. Though He has naught, His words make it so.'" The boy turns back to look into the Master's loving gaze. "So if you tell me to give them water to drink, I will do so, for your word has power."

"How much power?" questions the Master.

Ladle tipping and splashing water onto the ground, the boy scratches his head. "I am not sure, but I think a great deal because you show me you have no coin, no food, you wear no signet of office, yet all these follow you. You must be a great man."

"Let me ask you this … Of all the things that you would ask of God this day, what would be the first, my son?"

"Do you say to me, good sir, that your word is heard by God?"

"I say naught to you, but a question. Can you answer it?" The Master laughs.

One of the Apostles takes the ladle from the fidgeting boy since he is clearly struggling to figure out what this man is asking of him.

He looks about a bit, then his face brightens and his eyelids lift, almost into the hair hanging down over his brow. "Well, you have asked, so here is my answer. I would ask that she," turning to point at his mother, "be brought back into joy. That is what I would ask."

"Does she wish to be joyful?" the Master asks, glancing at the Apostles.

"Oh yes, I am certain she does."

"May I hear her speak it?"

"You mean my mother?"

"Is it not she of whom we speak?" the Master answers, stifling a laugh.

"Oh, yes! Just a moment." He races over to his mother, pointing and talking. She shakes her head. He talks and talks, waving his arms and pointing to the food, and pointing to the entourage. His head hanging, he walks slowly back to the Master. "She cannot come and ask you. She is too embarrassed."

"About what?" the Master asks.

"Many things. She has followed paths that are … well, she calls them dark."

"There is no path upon which the light of God does not shine. Tell her that. And tell her that I, Jesus, have said it."

The woman's hands come up to cover her face, and her body rocks, wracked with her sobbing. Something, somehow, has touched her. Her children scurry as they see her struggle, trying to rise to her feet.

Stiffly, but with some brightness, she makes her way to Jesus. Bent over, still covering most of her face, she extends her hand. "I know your name."

"I thought it might be so," Jesus answers, "For I remember that he has passed this way, has he not?"

"Yes. Long ago. His medicines are gone, and now my body has returned to its state of dis-ease and pain. But he said that one day the light of God might come this way. And he said, embracing me as he did, 'When you see that light, go unto it, and ask it, and He, Jesus, will give it unto thee. And where mine herbs and such have made thee well and whole for a time, He will make you well and whole for all time.'" Struggling, almost falling over, she tries to kneel. "As the soothsayer encouraged me, so do I ask it of you, O Jesus, Light of God, say but the word, and I am whole."

The Apostles and many others ring them. Many are in awe, for they have not seen, as some, the healing of Justus, or the guardian, or the other works that the Master is said to have done.

Jesus bends and extends His hand, placing His palm atop her head. He whispers softly, "Thy sins are no more. Give unto them that which is their direction to leave thee, and receive this." His fingers tighten just a bit. "Here is the bread of life. Here is the light of God. According to thy faith, so is it given thee.

"Arise, sweet sister, and be whole. Thou art Teresa, the living light of God."

In the mind of the faithful, ever is there the question: Is a path that leads unto darkness, in truth, too distant from those that lead unto light? Or are they as good brethren that, though they know it not, travel upon the same great path, believing their way to be different and divergent, and yet, it is not?

If thou wouldst guide them and thou knowest these things to be true – that there are not many paths, but only the belief in them and thus the movement into them as they are created through that belief – then is it as it is asked of thee, that thou canst give it in the strength of the truth of God. So knowing, as thou givest it, believe unto it, that they would see thy belief and know it to be good and righteous. Thereafter, as Teresa asked our Lord, ask, "Give it unto me that I, too, might be whole and well, and that I might be that cup in which there would live evermore eternal testimony unto You." So did she ask, so was it given.

But look. Look with great care, love, reverence, and thine own personal oneness with all that has gone before: Many gave all that they had to prepare the Way that the Master might enter and find it passable. And that they could offer the gifts – the treasures most sacred, most precious unto them as individual Children of God – knowing that as they offered these, He would see it and know it to be the goodness that was resident within Him, as well. Together, they gave it name, and they spoke that name, and it became a part of the gift of the Promise.

And thus, He comes!

Chapter Fourteen

After the Light

Her eyelids flutter open. The first impact of what she sees resonates within … empty, hollow, as though only a shell of what was present remains. Her breath, sharply drawn in, seems to sting as the realization of all that happened hits her. She struggles to shrug off the Master's departure, yet it lies heavily upon her as though a great weight were suppressing her own breathing, in and out. She struggles to normalize it, feeling her body's dullness, an ache, a bit of pain, stiffness in the legs and arms, knowing full well these are nuances of the emotional impact. Knowing full well that the journey must continue, the work yet lies ahead. For His message, His truth, and, yes, His light now rests as a mantel upon the shoulders of those with whom He has shared and given so very much.

She looks across the room, dimly lit by the embers of the evening's last fire, and perceives her Sisters, some of whom are stirring, several sitting glassy-cyed, peering at the embers on the hearth. Hannah brings herself up as best she can to a seated position and, drawing up her knees, places her head upon them, her chin struggling to find a comfortable position between them, her arms locking around her legs. She begins to rock, feeling the flow of the tears as they well up. Her heart leaps here and there with the memory of her Brother who has gone.

The chamber is filled with the faithful: the Expectant Ones and all who have become associated with them. Indeed, in many other locations similar groups gather, for no one place can hold them all. But here in the house of James and John, we see a man leaning back in a corner, head bowed and covered with the layers of his outer garment. Although his eyes are open, he is looking down, seeing naught, as though he were not present in the sense of being alive, but that his mind and spirit have gone on, leaving behind only the shell of this sizable one who has become known as the Rock.

Some of the others have apparently dozed off, exhausted by the emotion and the strain and the physical demands that the last several days have made. Some are staring up at the ceiling. The rest glance about aimlessly.

The embers on the hearth occasionally flicker into tiny flames, for it is broad and deep. Yet, none rises to refuel it, seemingly preferring the dim, warm light being cast by the final vestiges of the spent fire.

His head comes up, and his eyes blink as he looks into the flames that have sprung up towards the rear. His mind is reeling with the events of the last several days. He smiles inwardly at the realization that his own heart feels like the name given to him … his heart feels like a rock.

Without thinking, Peter slowly and quietly gets to his feet and, with careful, measured steps, walks over to the edge of the hearth. Bending down, he grasps some of the cold ash scattered around the periphery of the fire. He straightens up, and holding the ash as he works it to and fro with his fingers, his hand becomes blackened. Ever so slowly and deliberately, he raises his hand to his face and slowly spreads the ash all over it, his eyes again dull, his hand moving slowly, rubbing, feeling his face as he covers it. He places his forearm against the mantel and leans his head upon it, gazing into the embers below. He stands there for some time. Then he feels a soft touch upon his left shoulder.

Instantly a flood of realizations courses throughout his being, and a collage of memories races through his mind at dizzying speed. Unable to process them, he lifts his head and shakes it, then turns to look into the warm, loving eyes of Mary.

They gaze at one another for long moments in silence. Here and there, several of the other Maidens note this and are watching carefully, lovingly. His ashen hand rises without a thought, and he places it on Mary's hand, which still rests upon his shoulder. The dusty ash that he has spread upon his face flakes off here and there, and She raises Her other hand to brush the ash from beneath his eyes.

"All is forgiven," She whispers softly. "You know this. Before it came to pass, even then, was it already forgiven, else He would not have said it to you, but to tell you that He knew it. Yet, then and now, does His love flow to you. If you dwell in your current place of sorrow, and if you hold onto that which is your feeling of betrayal of Him, know you not that you close yourself off from Him? You, of all who followed Him, did He recognize and honor." She reaches to grasp a portion of the hem of Her robe, lifts it, and begins to wipe the ash from Peter's face.

His facial muscles twitch, divulging the struggle taking place within him. He swallows. His eyes flutter as he attempts to stay the flood of emotion, the array of thoughts he has held in these last hours and minutes.

She leads him by the arm as one would a child and gestures for him to seat himself. She turns to look into the eyes of Her sister Andra, who has brought a bowl of warm tea. Nodding and smiling to one another, Mary turns with the bowl in her hands, holding it out for Peter. "Drink of this. Think of Him as you do, and let the warmth of this tea and our love for you remind you of what is within you that awaits being called forth, what is to be your gift as He has given it unto you. Honor that and honor yourself, as He has so done."

Peter looks up into Her warm face and glances at Andra, whose customary stoicism and authority are softened by the flow of love given unto a brother who is in need. This, as much as the warmth that might be well anticipated from Our Lady, seems to revitalize him. With one hand holding the bowl of tea, he extends his blackened hand to Andra. She glances down at it and then into Peter's eyes, now wide, filled with the willingness to receive from these beautiful Maidens whose lives have been dedicated to giving. She breaks into a smile as she bends to take the great ashen hand into her own and kisses it.

We can barely make out that it is a body. At first glance, it appears to be a pile of outer garments tossed casually into the corner of the room. But here and there, we can see the movement of some of them as they pulse up and down, indicating a form beneath them, and that the form is softly sobbing. Finally an arm comes up and sweeps the covering from her head, exposing the face of Little Mary. Hers is the position furthest from the hearth and the flame, and one might reason that this is why she shudders, as though cold. But the coldness lies in her heart, with the emptiness she feels, for that which she has loved most in this life has been taken from it. Her cheeks are dry, for there are no more tears to flow down them. Her jaw juts forward, indicative of the clenched nature of the struggle going on within her. While her eyes are awide and moving about the room, there is no light in them, nor any indication that they recognize anything they see. It is like watching one whose thoughts are elsewhere and whose body and sight are merely automated reactions, outcroppings of the life force within but with none of the heart and none of the spirit's light.

Eloise studies her sister carefully. She understands, for she, too, feels this same call within. She shifts her focus as she and the other sisters were carefully, lovingly trained to do, and closing out the sight of Little Mary for a moment,

Eloise seeks. Doing so, she feels the Comforter that each of the Maidens holds within, and she asks, *It is I, Thy sister Eloise. Guide Thou me that I might know how to serve this light of my spirit, this joy of my heart, which glows eternally, as I know it shall. Tell me, sweet Father, how do I serve my sister Mary?* Her face brightens. Her eyes open, round with wonder. *I will do this, my Lord.*

Straightening herself and sitting upright, she brings her hands together over her heart and begins to rock this way and that. At first, one can only hear, barely audible, a single sweet tone. Then it grows, and the more it does, the more she sways left and right, her eyes filled with the light of God's guidance.

Little Mary's head turns sharply to see where the sound is coming from, incongruous with the event that has followed. At first, she wants to say, *Hold thy tongue, sister. Thou blasphemest!* But as her eyes connect with Eloise's, she sees and remembers with a flood of light and a surge of warmth. All her many tensed muscles begin to relax as they bathe in the love and sisterhood of her sweet Eloise. At first a flicker, then the corner of Little Mary's mouth turns up, as is so common for her. All of her Sisters know that her smile is sharp to one side, and lesser to the other. So much so that she has always countered anyone who mentioned this by saying, "This side points towards God, the other side brings God into the Earth." She begins to sway. Her face brightened, her hands come up, and she, too, places them, in the Maiden's tradition, over her heart. Soon her clear, beautiful voice adds her own tone to that of Eloise.

Across the way, we hear Editha creating a chord with the other two, and now Hannah, Abigale, all of them lift up their faces and add their voices to what is a beautiful, undulating embrace of sound.

He walks brusquely through the portal into the commander's chambers. The commander looks at him with anticipation so intense it seems to fill the entire room. Utterly out of character, the captain does not salute. He has removed his headgear and placed it underneath his right arm, yet it remains hanging down, as though lifeless.

"I have been waiting for you. Report! Is it completed?"

The captain's jaw works this way and that, his eyebrows pinched together as he strives to find some way to speak.

The commander, seeing this and noting that the captain has not saluted, leans back studying him. "Well?"

"It is completed."

"How many of the others did you gather? I want all of the potential troublemakers silenced once and for all. They can join their so-called king in his new kingdom, wherever that might be."

The commander's words sting the captain. His facial contortions register this and affect even the stoic and prideful commander, who longs only to return to Rome to be honored, perhaps even with a place in the Senate. His face goes white as the captain wordlessly reaches up and unbuckles first one side of his armor and then the other, his eyes fixed upon the commander, his face rigid with the tension of its twitching muscles.

The thud of his armor hitting the floor echoes in the stillness of the room. He remains silent as he slips the helmet from underneath his arm and places it on the table before the commander. Then, from under his tunic, he withdraws a small parchment, holding it forth in his outstretched arm. "I am tending my resignation. I have served Rome faithfully for these past many years. Above all else, I believe you well know, my commander, I have done so with honor. Beyond this point, I cannot serve honorably. Therefore, I have chosen as a freeborn citizen of Rome to resign my position."

The previously ashen face of the commander becomes, unbelievably, even more so. He twists and turns, trying to find words with which to respond. For here is one of his most trusted captains, one whose last several decades of life have been dedicated to the pursuit of the troublemakers, of those who would resist, of those who strive to build, as they call it, the Kingdom of God here in this area that is his to command! So often he heard and saw the vengeful hatred this same man spit out in moments of rage and frustration as he sought to find those called the Expectant Ones and was repeatedly thwarted one way or another.

Shaking with disbelief and the surge of emotion that follows, the commander rises to his feet. With slow, marked control, he places his hands on the table between them and pitches forward a fraction of a meter from the captain's rigid face. "I do not believe what I am hearing and seeing!"

He steps back and begins to pace, turning occasionally to glare at the captain as he tries to find the words that will command a change in his captain's new, seemingly resolute position. "This is the fruition of your quest, Captain. You should see this as the ultimate success of your service. Rome will honor you greatly, I have no doubt. Indeed, if you will, place your armor back on, and I will send you to Rome on the morrow, where you and your company can be honored appropriately for stopping this uprising once and for all."

The captain does not respond.

"Have you gone deaf, man? Do you not grasp what I am offering you? Stature, wealth, freedom, perhaps positions, untold positions. Perhaps even command of a legion. Or greater! The honor awaits you, and the recognition that Rome will bestow upon you ... you, sir, will be remembered forever! Children will sing songs about you. Poets will write odes to your name and your works. You can even take those you have gathered of His followers to Rome with you as living testaments, bringing you more great wealth, for, indeed, they would be purchased from you. What say you, Captain? Speak man!"

The captain's head drops as he searches for words, as

though he might find them written on the floor of the commander's chamber. Seeing none, he lifts his face to fix his eyes on the commander's, which are flashing with incredulity and stupefaction. "I have none to take, Commander."

"What?"

"Let me tell you of what transpired. As you ordered, I took my men and during the event we wandered, carefully studying the entire crowd, the throng, many multitudes. You cannot imagine how many came. They might perhaps yet be gathered, even as we speak.

"When one of my soldiers pierced His side with a lance, I expected them to curse the man for it. Yes, I expected Him to curse the soldier too, prophet or not! But He only gave a small cry and then ..." The captain's gaze returns momentarily to the floor. "Sir, I heard Him say to my soldier, 'I forgive you.'

"I looked around. None were cursing him. None raised their fists. None fomented any aggressive action against any of us. I tell you, Commander, in that moment, we could have had a rebellion that would have reached your very quarters, for the multitude was that great, and had they desired to so do, they could have easily overwhelmed us and the entire garrison. And you, sir! They could have come here by the hundreds, by the thousands, and taken you from these quarters to that dreary mount and placed you and me there, just as we placed Him. And they could, as well, have thereupon pierced our sides with a lance.

"But, sir, I looked into their eyes and saw no hatred. I heard no threats, no cursing us. I tell you, some even were singing softly! Then, I looked about and saw some of my own men cast off their weapons, loosen their armor, and walk away, I am sure, never to be seen again.

"The power that I felt, sir, seemed to equal the power of my own emotion of hatred and anger, as I pursued these very people for decades. And here they were. For the first time, I saw them. And I saw Him.

"Could I have brought any back to you as you ordered, any whose hearts bore treason and rebellion? No, sir. These hearts hold only love and peace, and if there is anything they would do unto us and even Rome itself, I would have to call it goodness. For none ... I say to you, none of these His followers had even a moment's flicker, not a moment, of hostility or anger toward me or my men. So do I report. These are as a remarkable flock of sheep whose shepherd has left them.

"I wish nothing further from Rome, but that which is my birthright ... my freedom. I mean you no disrespect, sir, and ask only that you respect my request, remembering the many years I have faithfully and honorably served you and Rome. I await your decision."

The stillness in the chamber seems to have substance, as though one could gather it up and jar it, so thick is the energy of disbelief and wonder. And the captain emanates a light, an essence, never before seen by the commander. Indeed, in many respects, were it not for the difference in station, the two could have been brothers.

It is from this sense of brotherhood that the commander once again leans on his table to look into the captain's unblinking eyes, in disbelief and yet in wonder. "I respect that which you have stated, and know you for your honor and your truthfulness. Thus it is without question that I receive your report and shall take no action for your failure to bring other rebels to the garrison. But I say to you once more, not just as your commander, but as a fellow-at-arms remembering the many tasks you have performed for Rome and me with valor, reconsider your decision. Take a fortnight's leave and enjoy the foods and other pleasures that await you and your station. At the fortnight's end, come, and we shall speak of this then."

Again, the silence is tangible.

The captain's words seem like objects floating about on a

sea of the silence as he responds. "Commander, I thank you. But I give you this final salute, for my decision stands. In my heart now is only the desire to know myself, and that which His eyes have awakened within me. For I tell you, as I walked beneath Him to chastise my soldier for his action, I glanced up at Him. His eyes were open. I saw no fear, no horror of death approaching swiftly to descend upon Him. I did, though, see something I must find. All else has fallen away, sir, but this light that is now in my heart, which His words to me ignited there." The captain bows his head.

After a pause, the commander can no longer help but inquire, "What were these words that have so enchanted you?"

The captain raises his head. His eyes are now soft and round, his face relaxed and smiling. "He said, sir, 'I shall make a place for thee.'"

The rectangular chamber within Nicodemus' home is sizeable, yet, there is barely room to walk about. Here, there, all about, there are individuals in varying positions, some bobbing up and down in prayer as is the custom, with a prayer cloth draped over them. Others have lit a bit of incense, and its fragrance hangs like a blue haze just above their heads. Several of the Maidens who have come to honor and tend to Nicodemus and the household have busied themselves preparing foods.

There is a knock upon the portal.

As Nicodemus turns to look, his servant moves quickly. Peering through the small opening on the door, she speaks softly. The darkness of nightfall is so thick and heavy that naught can be seen without a flame, but she receives an appropriate response. She opens the door, bending and cautiously looking around its edge to be certain that she has discerned correctly. Several elderly guardians of the Expectant Ones have moved to position themselves nearby, should they be needed. Their aged hands and worn knuckles firmly grasp their stout staffs as they have for so many decades, ready as ever to use them.

He strides into the forechamber. In the glow of the hearth fire, he appears to be one of wealth and stature. The fine embroidery and ribbing around his head covering catches a flicker of light. The multiple layers of his garments are unsullied by the dust and grime of travel, but appear freshly cleaned, as does he.

Arms upstretched, Nicodemus hurries to greet him. "Oh, Joseph, what joy to have you here! You honor my abode. Come! The others will be so reassured that you are here."

As Joseph of Arimathea is announced, many draw near to bless him and thank him. He moves about to converse with many whom he has seen but rarely over the past decades. Finally, he comes to take a position of honor as a guest in the home of Nicodemus. Several of those who have come from the household of Zebedee are gathered with him.

"We will ask for Him, then," James begins.

"Yes." Joseph moves so Nicodemus may seat himself at his side. "All is prepared, all is at the ready."

"Do you think they will honor our request?"

Turning to answer the younger Nathanael, Nicodemus nods and smiles. "I believe we can express it in a way that will be no threat whatsoever to them. We have prepared a place of honor and respect in which to receive Him. A number of the Maidens have prepared the cloth and ointments. Indeed, all is at the ready." Nicodemus casts a careful glance around at those who are now gathered about them at the table, some standing in pockets two and three deep.

"And the prophesies? What think you, Nicodemus?" James asks quietly.

"He has said it, and it has been prophesied. We can do only what we know to do, and have all of this arranged. What shall follow is in their hands." He looks up. "And God's."

They look carefully into the flame as several of the new maidens fuel it and stir the contents of the great pot being heated above it. Those who have remained because of their inability to journey are positioned close to the flame to absorb its warmth.

"It is time for the work to begin anew," Zelotese avows softly.

"Indeed." Iliam's face is blank.

With considerable effort, Judy raises herself and smiles, glancing at Zelotese. Her face displays her many years of service, though the small wrinkles in her skin could in no way diminish her beauty. "Would that we could join you, brother," she offers softly, turning and glancing at Anna's equally warm and aged countenance. "Our days are few here, and we joyfully anticipate seeing Him again. But know this, dear brothers, as He has said unto all of us and to so many, *I am always with you.* So, too, am I and my sweet sister ever with you, as well.

"Now, as He oft reminded us, His light must be carefully sown into the hearts and minds of those who will follow, that they might bear it forth, and that it might grow and brighten, bringing hope, forgiveness, and love to those who lie ahead on the journey called life."

Judy's slender forearm rises as she places her palm over her heart. We hear her and her sister Anna echo simple, but powerful words. "The peace of God be with thee."

$$\big\uparrow$$

We shall conclude these works here. As we so do, we remind any who may hear them that what we have chosen to give unto the Earth in this recounting, we give in absolute humbleness and utter service to the Word of God in the form called Christ.

Know ye well everyone: The Word of God is within you, not apart, nor distant, nor gone, but ever with you. Thus is it our humble prayer that what has been given will give you, just as it gave that captain, cause to search joyfully. For, indeed, He makes a place for thee, as well.

We give thanks unto all those forces which have come forward and offered this information in the individual and collective sense, and we give thanks unto God for the joy of this humbling service. May the grace and blessings of our Father's wisdom ever be as a lamp to guide your footsteps.

Fare thee well, dear friends.

Epilogue

And He Shall Call Them

Jacob's passing was by his own choice. Upon the mount called Lookout, he passed with the closure of day, setting his own spirit free to soar up into the embrace of the darkness of night.

Iliam followed the path with those who were carrying the works and teachings forward, performing healings for those who sought them, until that time as his body became weary. He then called out and was lifted up by those with whom he served in that lifetime. And these are those here, speaking.

Eloise, Sarah, and all of the Sisters made their way slowly, purposefully, back along the pathway on which the Master walked and taught and did His works, first, into the wilderness, then to the Three Holy Mountains, and finally to the Sacred Spring of healing. Here, they celebrated, gave thanks unto God, and performed their sacred dance one last time. Upon its completion, they paused to pray, to break bread, to sip wine. Gazing at the dimming fire and the sky's light glistening on the water of the Healing Spring, they clasped hands and departed. They were received by those whom their loving hands had nurtured. He lifted them up in His gladness.

Each of the others, including the guardians and the ancient teachers, was equally embraced as they, too, were met at the point of crossing in their own time. And each was given according to that which they had wrought in that lifetime.

Such a glorious coming together and rejoicing followed that, even now, it can be heard by those who travel forth with gladness of heart. There came to pass that period of time wherein the spirits of their eternal nature came to know themselves once again in the completeness of their faith. And in this knowing, that faith grew. In the growth of that united faith, a marker was placed in the heavens that all who would seek might be illuminated by it, and their path made open and passable. Yet does it shine!

There followed, then, the movement on the part of the individuals and groups to continue on with the Promise and the service unto those who were seeking to carry the Word forward, that ever would there be one who might fall and ask, and raising up a hand, there would be one ready to clasp it and lift them up.

Then came those times when some of the Expectant Ones moved back into positions of direct service to the Earth, while others chose to move into the Earth by taking on physical form and doing various works.

As would naturally be expected, after the Master's life was no longer seen and known through personal experience, personal memory, turmoil ensued, and conflict, and challenge upon challenge … Yet, ever, the Expectant Ones walked the

Earth, seeking to continue the Word and the peace. All the while, there were those overseers and elders whose positions were made even more glorious and joyful, as they had served with and walked with the Master. So here, then, they joined with the one who guards the Path and the Way, Lord Michael, that there could be prepared an opportunity when the Path was ready and those who bore the Mark might awaken, that from that awakening, there would be the manna, the nourishment, of their spirits. Then they would send those who were to mingle with those in the flesh ... some to take on flesh themselves, and others to walk in their midst silently.

And the Master called forth the light once again and set it in place at 2:01 AM Eastern Standard Time, January 11, two-ought-ought-ought, to remain to an approximate time, 2018. It was preparatory to a greater shift in consciousness, which could be adjudged as the first of seven steps to the kingdom of the throne of God: Seven great Waves of Light did He put before the world ... the steps for them to return to oneness with God.

Some gathered together that their lives might be all the brighter and that their truth and their faith would be a beacon of hope and promise to others. Others, yet afar and near, would do the same in their own teaching in their own way and manner.

Thus will come that time when the gates will open and the paths will be made aright. He will stand before them with gladness in His heart. And He shall call them.

Upon His entry, there will be a call. Those who are seeking, those who are choosing, will be called unto Him, and they will walk beside Him as colleagues, as brother and sister … as one.

Thereafter, will be that intent to prepare the way and make it passable for those souls who are awakening, those who have found forgiveness and hope and grace.

These, then, when the time is aright, will enter and become those who bear the Promise unto the Thousand Years of Peace.

– Lama Sing

ABOUT LAMA SING

More than thirty years ago, for our convenience, the one through whom this information flows accepted the name Lama Sing, though it was stated they, themselves, have no need for names or titles.

"We identify ourselves only as servants of God, dedicated to you, our brothers and sisters in the Earth."

–Lama Sing

ↅ

ABOUT THIS CHANNEL

"Channel is that term given generally to those who enable themselves to be, as much as possible, open and passable in terms of information that can pass through them from the Universal Consciousness or other such which are not associated in the direct sense with their finite consciousness of the current incarnation."

–Lama Sing

BOOKS BY AL MINER & LAMA SING

The Chosen: *Backstory to the Essene Legacy*
The Promise: *Book I of The Essene Legacy*
The Awakening: *Book II of The Essene Legacy*
The Path: *Book III of The Essene Legacy*

In Realms Beyond: *Book I of The Peter Chronicles*
In Realms Beyond: *Study Guide*
Awakening Hope: *Book II of The Peter Chronicles*
Return to Earth: *Book III of The Peter Chronicle*

Death, Dying, and Beyond:
  How to Prepare for The Journey Vol I
The Sea of Faces:
  How to Prepare for The Journey Vol II

Jesus: *Book I*
Jesus: *Book II*

The Course in Mastery

When Comes the Call

Seed Thoughts
Seed Thoughts to Consciousness

Stepstones: Compilation 1

The "Little Book" Series:
  The Children's Story

ABOUT AL MINER

A chance hypnosis session in 1973 began Al's tenure as the channel for Lama Sing. Since then, nearly 10,000 readings have been given in a trance state, answering technical and personal questions on such topics as science, health and disease, history, geophysical, spiritual, philosophical, metaphysical, past and future times, and much more. The validity of the information has been substantiated and documented by research institutions and individuals, and those receiving personal readings continue to refer others to Al's work based on the accuracy and integrity of the information in their readings. In 1984, St. Johns University awarded Al an honorary doctoral degree in parapsychology.

Al is no longer accepting requests for personal readings, but, rather, is devoting his remaining time to works intended to be good for all. Much of his current research is dedicated to the concept that the best of all guidance is that which comes from within. Al lives with his wife in Florida.

You can read more about Al's life and works at the Lama Sing website: *www.lamasing.net*.